Peter and Irene,

Hope you enjoy the best. all the best.

Rich

RICH
THAT'S
RICH
THAT'S
RICH
THAT'S
RICH

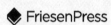 FriesenPress

One Printers Way
Altona, MB R0G 0B0
Canada

www.friesenpress.com

ISBN
978-1-03-832262-3 (Hardcover)
978-1-03-832261-6 (Paperback)
978-1-03-832263-0 (eBook)

1. BIOGRAPHY & AUTOBIOGRAPHY, POLITICAL

Distributed to the trade by The Ingram Book Company

THAT'S RICH

the Rise and Fall
of the BC Liberals

A Biography of
Rich Coleman

JUDI TYABJI

Photo Credits:

Cover G Wilson 1991 debate
Global News October 2, 202: B.C. election: Leaders' debate set for Oct. 13
See Keith Baldrey video at about the 1 minute mark

Cover G Campbell in rally
Globe & Mail November 3, 2010: Political life of B.C. Premier Gordon Campbell.
Caption: B.C. Liberal Leader Gordon Campbell arrives at a Vancouver television
station for an election debate in 1996. CHUCK STOODY/THE CANADIAN PRESS

Cover G Campbell at Olympics
Globe & Mail November 3, 2010: Political life of B.C. Premier Gordon Campbell.
Caption: Premier Gordon Campbell makes a speech during the official
Olympics lighting ceremony outside the BC legislative assembly in Victoria
October 30, 2009. JOHN LEHMANN

Cover G Wilson in debate
Globe & Mail August 17, 2017: B.C.'s former LNG advocate sues John Horgan for
defamation. Caption: A February, 2000, file photo of former B.C. Liberal leader
Gordon Wilson. ADRIAN WYLD/THE CANADIAN PRESS

Cover C Clark K Falcon
Google links to this article for origin of image Globe & Mail February 10, 2011:
How to win friends (not really) and influence enemies (a little)

Cover G Wilson C Clark
CBC News August 12, 2017: B.C. minister apologizes to Gordon Wilson for
comments about work performance. Caption: Gordon Wilson with Christy
Clark during a photo op at YVR in 2013. (CBC)

Cover Clark and Coleman at LNG announcement
BC Government, uploaded Nov. 4, 2016. https://www.flickr.com/photos/
bcgovphotos/30662019752/in/album-72157663031227621/

K Falcon
CityNews November 13, 2022: BC Liberal members to vote on name change.
Caption: BC Liberal Party members can vote on whether or not to change the
name of the party to "BC United." Photo Courtesy: BC Liberal Party

Photos on page 129, 130, 131, 132, 133, 134, 135, 136, 137, 138, 139, 140, 141, 142
BC government's photo collection on Flickr. All images are available for re-use
under the Creative Commons License Attribution-NonCommercial-NoDerivs

Other three photos are supplied by Michele Coleman

Dedication

This book is dedicated to Allan Gregory, Battalion Chief for Vancouver Fire and Rescue Services (VFRS), and the people like him. Gregory has taught me more about First Responders and their commitment to service than I learned in my many decades of community and political engagement. He is the epitome of a hardworking and committed firefighter, showing up for the people he serves during one of the most challenging times since VFRS started in 1886. He and his colleagues continue to serve even as cancer rates and mental health issues challenge firefighters and their families. I dedicate this book as a small part in recognizing the work that he and others like him do to protect us all, every day, as foundational to our civil society.

Acknowledgements

As with my previous books, I have considerable gratitude for the efficient, professional, and friendly assistance provided by Erika Luebbe of the BC Legislative library. I am in awe of her ability to provide quick data that I can weave into my books, and it's been almost 25 years since my first request. I also want to thank my good friend, the talented and hardworking April White, who allowed me to bunk with her in Mexico to write while she created another Haida art masterpiece. It was a fun and productive time of sunsets, laughter, memories, and a finished manuscript.

Table of Contents

Introduction
THAT'S RICH

There is no lack of readers and listeners; it is for us to produce something worth being written and heard.

—Pliny the Younger

This is my fourth and final book on BC politics, unless, like Cher, I just keep on doing farewell tours. It has been 30 years since my first book. While it is possible there will be a fifth book, it would almost certainly have to be about the same timeframe as this one, because that's the timeframe I know best. Like Cher, I would only keep going if I could write about my greatest hits.

My first book, published in 1994, focused on Gordon Wilson. It was more about issues than partisan politics. My second book was about NDP leader Glen Clark, the third about Liberal leader Christy Clark, and this one is about a conservative, Rich Coleman. By the end of this book, all four of these characters are dancing in the same sector of free enterprise, with Glen Clark second in command to BC's best-known self-made billionaire, Jimmy Pattison.

This book is my attempt to do justice to the rise and fall of the BC Liberals. I also had a very personal perspective on this, since in 1991 I was elected to the political party that would be renamed "BC Liberals" in 1994. I will not go into enormous detail about the events leading up to that. For my perspective on that, you can read my first book on politics, *Political Affairs*. Later in this book,

I will touch on the name change and the context, because it is relevant to the person whose life provides the perspective for the full journey of the BC Liberals: from inception, through growth, to government, then opposition, and then obscurity. How does a party appear from almost nowhere, govern a wealthy province for 16 years, and then disappear a few years after its government falls?

How does a provincial Liberal Party become irrelevant in one of Canada's most populous provinces even as the federal Liberal Party governs the country?

The book is about Rich Coleman and his 24 years of elected service as an MLA, cabinet minister, Deputy Premier, and interim party leader. It is not possible to do justice to everything that he accomplished in one book, nor can I expand my focus to the government at large. Instead, Coleman is the everyman who can take us on this journey so we can see what he did, how he did it, and how the public encountered it. I will leave it for others to go into depth about the government as a whole, or other key players.

The focus is from 1987 until 2023, with a conclusion that might be relevant in the election of 2024. I never imagined I would write even one book about politics, much less politics in BC—however, the more I feel the impact of bad government, and the more I listen to my adult children talk about housing, the price of food, mental health issues, and the impact of wildfires, the more motivated I am to engage people in a conversation about who is in charge of the decisions that impact us all. The eternal optimist, I hope that the more people know, the more motivated they will be to get involved in solving the problems and showing up for elections. One can always hope, right?

My father, Alan Tyabji, was a supporter of the Social Credit Party in Kelowna from the time we moved there in 1973 until I entered politics as a Liberal in 1988, and even then, he worked closely with the Social Credit government on grape and wine policy. My mother, Christine Quinter (née Ritchin), was a passionate supporter of the NDP. Their votes would cancel each other out in every provincial election, and the discussions at home about the two parties' policies were pretty colourful. My mum could have written ads for the NDP to recruit votes.

My parents provided me with a very personal perspective on the enormous divide between Social Credit and NDP supporters, and like most BC voters, I really didn't pay too much attention until it was time to vote, and I often voted based on the candidate. Then at 23 when my son was six weeks old, I was talked into becoming a candidate, and I started to pay attention. Over the decades since, I have sometimes run away from the mayhem of BC politics, and other times been drawn back in.

My second book, *Daggers Unsheathed: the Political Assassination of Glen Clark* (2002), was about NDP Premier Glen Clark. In it I walked readers through much of the NDP's governing years from 1991 to 2001. My third book, *Christy Clark: Behind the Smile* (2016) was about BC Liberal Premier Christy Clark. At the end of this book on Coleman we will have an insight into the final chapters of the Christy Clark government and beyond, into the early days of the minority NDP government. My wish for readers of BC politics is that this book on Rich Coleman adds additional insights into the years I have already covered, and the years I have not really covered, which were the years when Gordon Campbell was leader of the BC Liberals and Rich Coleman was one of his senior cabinet ministers.

2020 was a challenging year, as the COVID-19 virus took hold across the globe and changed the world. There were many other news stories that captured our attention, including the American election that saw—eventually—a Biden presidency replace Trump's, and a national focus on Canada's response to Covid, with Prime Minister Justin Trudeau providing daily live news updates. In British Columbia, a minority NDP government called a general election with the lowest voter turnout in history, with about half the ballots sent in by mail. The NDP won their first majority government since 1996, with little fanfare, while many BC Liberal Members of the Legislative Assembly decided to retire. A majority government with over HALF the votes sent in by mail—this would have been an unimaginable situation in most previous elections.

In 2020, Rich Coleman was one of the politicians who decided to retire from politics. He had served for 24 years and was not inspired by the leadership of the BC Liberals at that time. His riding elected the NDP candidate, something few would have predicted even months earlier because Langley had been a staunchly conservative riding for decades.

Coleman's decision came after years of NDP MLAs targeting him, his office, and others in the BC Liberals with allegations about organized crime, money laundering, and other activities that led to the NDP government setting up the Cullen Commission in May 2019. November 2020's political news from BC captured the country's attention, with headlines including:

Editorial: Staggering allegations about money laundering at B.C. casinos, *Times-Colonist*, November 28, 2020;

Coleman, Heed ignored casino concerns, Cullen Hears, *The Vancouver Sun*, November 5, 2020;

Inquiry hears minister focused on money, not organized crime at B.C. casinos, *The Vancouver Sun* (online), November 5, 2020;

Ex-Mountie faces grilling from former minister's lawyer, repeats earlier testimony, *The Canadian Press*, November 17, 2020;

BC Liberals feared money-laundering crackdown would impact government revenue, *The Globe and Mail*, November 5, 2020;

Official dismissive of concerns of crime in casinos, commission hears, Mike Hager, *The Globe and Mail*, November 6, 2020.

Canada's premium national newspaper, *The Globe and Mail*, wrote:

> The provincial NDP government called the inquiry last May after three independent money-laundering reviews, including two by former deputy commissioner of the RCMP Peter German.
>
> Mr. German wrote of a "Vancouver model" of money laundering... (and) concluded: "High rollers from China facilitate the flight of capital from China using Canadian casinos, junket operations and investment in Canadian real estate."
>
> ...At the start of this year, B.C. Attorney General David Eby made it plain that a key objective of the money-laundering inquiry is to look into whether or how the former Liberal government let B.C. become a hotbed for transnational money laundering.[1]

Coleman testified in 2021 and Cullen reported out in 2022. One chapter of this book presents highlights of the Cullen Commission evidence and explains his findings. It is only one chapter because Coleman's 24-year career at MLA spanned so many issues and initiatives that reveal government and politics, from serial killer investigations to the response to 9/11, housing,

---

1   *B.C. feared money-laundering crackdown would hurt provincial revenue, Cullen Commission hears,* Mike Hager, *The Globe and Mail* (online), Toronto, ON, November 5, 2020.

wildfires, and public safety, that the inquiry was only a small piece of his time in office.

I never expected to be writing this book because I did not like Rich Coleman.

In early January of 2021 I received an email from him. Coleman was the former deputy premier and solicitor general and had served as a senior minister for the government of British Columbia for 16 years. The email was called "Book Writing" and it said, "I am no author. When you wrote *Behind the Smile*[2] why did you do it? Thanks."

My response? "Hi Rich, I did it because I am totally crazy… So many things that should be set straight when it comes to you."

I was referring to the high-profile headlines that connected Coleman to "staggering allegations of money laundering." There had been many news stories in the previous year. Although I didn't like Rich Coleman, I didn't believe the stories. In Coleman's 24 years of elected office, the one thing that came through for me was that he was almost painfully honest.

I had only talked to him a couple of times, although I had seen him in the news for many years. I knew we had very different political and personal views. He was a high-profile conservative, while I am a lifetime Liberal; Coleman was often in political stories with the group of male MLAs referred to, literally, as "knuckle draggers[3]," whereas I am known for being a fairly opinionated, progressive ethnic woman.

---

2   *Christy Clark: Behind the Smile*, with Heritage House Publishing was my
     third book on BC politics. I wrote *Daggers Unsheathed: the Political
     Assassination of Glen Clark* in 2002 with Heritage House, and *Political
     Affairs*, a look at the political journey of Gordon Wilson as Liberal leader,
     in 1994, with Horsdal and Schubart, which was acquired by
     Heritage House.

3   *'Knuckle draggers' aren't swaying Dosanjh*, Les Leyne, *Times-Colonist*, Victoria,
     BC, July 16, 1997.

After an email exchange, we spoke on the phone and I tried to recommend a good biographer for Coleman, but he insisted he wanted someone objective, and for the book to be similar to my first three. I pushed back that I was too busy, and then he used the phrase that nailed it: "I really want my grandchildren to know the truth about what I did." Sigh. As a grandmother myself, how could I resist that line?

I was asked once why I write my books, and I replied that writing them was a bit of a reflex: for example, if you see a baby about to crawl across a freeway, you don't stop to think whether you should grab it. You just grab the baby and make sure it is safe.

In this, my fourth book on BC politics, the baby is a 24-year record of public service as an elected Member of the Legislative Assembly (MLA), 16 years of which were as a senior cabinet minister—and there was a semi-truck barrelling down on that record.

I agreed to start the process, expecting that a few weeks in he would realize we would not get along; he would change his mind about trusting me with his story once he knew me better, and find an excuse to move to a biographer more like him. Instead, by the second interview my view of him turned upside down. It will take this book to explain that. I became hooked on the need to tell his story as part of the larger story of BC politics.

Rich Coleman was known as a social conservative. His name was in the media associated with claims that he opposed the rights of same-sex couples, including same-sex marriage. One of his close colleagues claimed he led a group of MLAs known as "the 13" who opposed abortion services.[4] He was generally seen as someone straight off the set of *Mad Men*, a popular show where powerful men ruled the corporate world with traditional 1960s values.

---

4   *Liberal MLA fears anti-abortionist infiltration of party*, Ted Nebbeling on John Hof of Campaign Life Coalition of BC, *Canadian Press NewsWire*, Toronto, ON, October 24, 1998.

Six-foot-three and heavy set, Coleman was a large and imposing figure who reported out like a police officer. He was often in
news conferences defending the Liberals for the latest "dirty deed"
as the Enforcer. He was unapologetic, blunt, and often came across
as pretty arrogant. There was seldom any kind of explanation
for why the BC Liberals were mucking about in some allegedly
nefarious activity.

I respected Coleman's years of service to the province and
knew he had an amazing track record when it came to affordable housing and natural gas development. As an observer of BC
politics, I did not have to like Coleman to know that the headlines
connecting him to organized crime and money laundering were
grossly unfair. As a political geek, I had read the details of the
reports behind the headlines, and there was a huge gap between
the evidence and the allegations.

This is a book about a man whose private personality is the
antithesis of his public image, and whose motivations to serve the
public and his family have been consistent before, during, and
after his time in elected office, from his early years as an RCMP
officer, through his time in business and with the Kinsmen, and
then his years as an elected member.

This book is written to protect a legacy that deserves to be
recorded and recognized, to share stories that otherwise would
remain untold, to provide outsiders a glimpse into the halls of
power, and to correct the public narrative.

That's Rich will take you behind the curtain of the BC Liberal
Party, starting in the late 1980s when the Social Credit Party started
to collapse, leading to a coalition of Liberals and Conservatives in
1994 under the leadership of Gordon Campbell. You will walk
through the rooms of the newly elected BC Liberal government,
seeing through the eyes of the Caucus Chair and Caucus Whip.
You will have a front-row seat to the response to the 9/11 attacks,
the investigation of a serial killer, the successful negotiation of a

Softwood Lumber Agreement, the creation of innovative affordable housing programs, the first State of Emergency called in response to BC wildfires, the only fully integrated police communication system in North America, and so much more. We will spend time with the former minister who walked Vancouver's Downtown Eastside alone at night, visiting his regular contacts there.

You will feel like you are in the room when the BC Liberal government falls and Coleman takes over as interim leader.

Was this a government connected to organized crime and money laundering, indifferent to the cost to the people and the role of good government? We will spend time with the man who was the kingmaker rather than the king and seek the answers.

THAT'S RICH

RICH

the Rise and Fall of the BC Liberals

Chapter 1
BC POLITICS

A nation can survive its fools, and even the ambitious. But it cannot survive treason from within. An enemy at the gates is less formidable, for he is known and carries his banner openly. But the traitor moves amongst those within the gate freely, his sly whispers rustling through all the alleys, heard in the very halls of government itself.

—Marcus Tullius Cicero

The westernmost of Canada's ten provinces, British Columbia occupies a massive amount of land—10% of Canada's total size and considerably more than either California or Florida[5]. BC is also a very wealthy province, and in the mid-1800s was flooded with fortune seekers pursuing gold along the Fraser River and up into the Cariboo region of the interior. Historically, the strong economy was built on the primary economic sector of forestry, mining, fishing, oil and gas, and agriculture; however, depletion of the fisheries and growing awareness of sustainability concerns led to changes in the resource sector governance in the 1990s. These changes began a diversification of the economy, a focus on value-added and manufacturing processes for the resource sector, and an

---

5   *How Big is British Columbia?*, BC *General Aviation Association*, BC, September 9, 2015.https://www.bcaviation.ca/september-09th-2015/

expansion of high technology, tourism, and entertainment sectors for a sustainable tertiary economy.

Politics in British Columbia has a historical randomness in terms of its political parties, personality politics, and voting patterns. Headline scandals and allegations of corruption against leaders have frequently driven a change in government or a shift in leadership, delivering new control to the levers of our resource-wealthy economy. As our economy evolved in the late twentieth century, moving away from mining and forestry toward development and tourism, BC's political dynamics shifted.

The BC Liberal Party re-emerged in 1991, knocking out a Social Credit dynasty and taking over official opposition status. The BC Liberals grew in strength in the 1996 election, then won a historic victory that almost destroyed the NDP in 2001. The BC Liberals ruled from 2001 until 2017, when Christy Clark won a minority government, missing a majority by 1 seat. The Green Party had a breakthrough in this election, with three MLAs in the legislature. The NDP and Green Party quickly made an agreement to knock the BC Liberals out of government in a non-confidence motion. It was supposed to be a coalition government, but in effect the Green Party handed the NDP a majority, which the NDP reinforced in 2020 during the COVID-19 pandemic, winning 57 of the 87 seats. The BC Liberal Party disappeared in 2023 when the party changed its name to the BC United Party.

Politics in BC is often difficult to follow. Which political party represents what? Which party can be trusted to fix certain issues? Why did a high-profile politician move to a completely different political party? Observers could get whiplash keeping up.

Rich Coleman was involved in the Social Credit Party in the 1991 election, was elected into the BC Liberal opposition in 1996, served as a senior cabinet minister for Gordon Campbell's government from 2001 to 2011, served as Deputy Premier for Christy Clark's government from 2011 to 2017, and took over as interim leader for the BC Liberals when they lost government to the NDP, staying on as MLA for his riding in Langley until the 2020 election. He won six consecutive elections, held many portfolios, and was the voice of the BC Liberals for much of their existence. This book will go behind the scenes of the BC Liberals from their inception to their collapse, sharing stories and insights from opposition to government to opposition to disappearance, through the voice and perspective of Rich Coleman and many of his colleagues—plus some Press Gallery comments.

BC's ever-changing political landscape has been a facet of our politics since before we joined the confederation of Canada in 1871, and the province's economic ties to the rich resource sector have often led to heated and high-stakes debates before, during, and after elections.

Throughout most of BC's history, there have been two political parties competing for power, and a simple analysis would say that one is "right wing" and business-oriented and one is "left wing" and labour-oriented. This is oversimplified, but it gives us a starting point for discussion. We will deconstruct it later. It is the business party that has more often changed its name, and the labour party that has more often changed its policies.

On the business side, there is an entrenched competition for power between those who would be considered Conservative and those who would be considered Liberal. Understanding the tension and frequent antagonism between the Conservative and Liberal factions is a key component in trying to follow BC's high-level power plays, because it is only when these two groups can work together that a pro-business party can be in government, and when this coalition fractures, power shifts to the opposing party. So far, neither the Conservative nor the Liberal leaders and supporters have ever opted to work with the labour party in any form of coalition.

Thinking of BC political parties as left wing and right wing is an extreme oversimplification, because BC has an identity that is also connected to environmental protection, small business development, remote wilderness, rural agriculture, the tech economy, and ethnic diversity, and these issues transcend the spectrum of right and left. For example, there was no fracture of the business coalition in 2017, yet the BC Liberals lost their majority. Why? This book will dive into that as part of the look behind the scenes.

It's style over substance, and timing, that helps with political success in BC. One common trait of the most successful leaders is their larger-than-life personas and populist approaches that connect in some way to all aspects of BC's identity, timed with political fatigue in the established parties. Personality politics has driven many election outcomes, rather than loyalty to a political party or ideology.

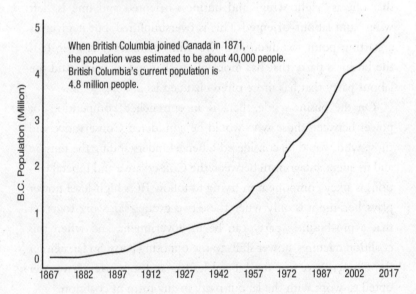

Long-term Change in British Columbia's Population Size (1867-2017)

When British Columbia joined Canada in 1871, the population was estimated to be about 40,000 people. British Columbia's current population is 4.8 million people.

Figure 1: BC's Population Change to 2017

The population of BC has grown steadily since confederation, and the rate of growth increased in the 1980s. Between 1986 and 2017, BC grew over 60% in population[6]. The voters, therefore, had little knowledge or allegiance to the existing political parties or leaders, many came from countries where English was not the dominant language, and the electorate was often volatile to indifferent about provincial elections.

As of September 2023, the population of British Columbia was over 5.3 million, an increase from 4.04 million in 2020.[7] In 2023, there were over 160,000 new international residents in British Columbia; meanwhile, many Canadian residents left to move to Ontario or Alberta. When these numbers are seen in the context of an election, it can really concentrate the actual number of voters who are ready, willing, and able to vote in a provincial election to a much smaller number. The collapse of the BC Liberal Party after the 2017 election and its disappearance in 2023 is going to add to the confusion for voters seeking the best option for a business-friendly government. How can you communicate to newcomers in any relevant way when your party has no track record in government?

6   *Trends in B.C.'s Population Size & Distribution*, Government of British Columbia, *Environmental Reporting BC*, March 2018. https://www.env.gov. bc.ca/soe/indicators/sustainability/bc-population.html

7   *Population Estimates for British Columbia, Canada, 2000-2022*, Government of British Columbia, *Statista Research Department*, October 2023. https://www.statista.com/statistics/569885/population-estimates-british-columbia-canada/

Chapter 2
LEADERSHIP
AND SCANDAL

The untrained mind keeps up a running commentary,
labelling everything, judging everything. Best to ignore that
commentary. Don't argue or resist, just ignore. Deprived of
attention and interest, this voice gets quieter and quieter and
eventually just shuts up.

—Plato

In a democracy, every voice has an equal opportunity to be heard through voting, and throughout BC political history, elections have been impacted by debates, scandal, and commentary that is frequently coloured by unfounded allegations. "Those who cannot remember the past are condemned to repeat it," as American philosopher George Santayana said[8]. Imagine how hard it is to remember a past that does not belong to you? In order for British Columbia to evolve out of its cycle of political randomness, the people have to have access to their past, the past inherited by virtue of adopting BC as their home. This is a large task and there are many historians better suited to take it on than I am; however, in order to set the stage for Rich Coleman's everyman journey

---

8   *The Life of Reason: Reason in Common Sense*, George Santayana, Scribner's, New York City, USA, 1905.

with the BC Liberals, this book attempts to give some context to the colourful and very interesting background to our politics.

From the first Governor of what would become BC through to the NDP Premier elected in 2020, strong personalities and focused determination have defined the province's best-known leaders. James Douglas, born in 1803 in Guyana, was a coloured[9] man who served as Governor from 1851 to 1864. Initially he governed only the Vancouver Island colony; later he took on the mainland of British Columbia, which at that time was a separate Crown colony. He is often called the "Father of British Columbia."[10] Douglas was a fur trader who rose to the level of Chief Factor with the Hudson Bay Company. The Hudson Bay Company was the most powerful organization in the Crown colonies of Vancouver Island and British Columbia, enriched by the fur trade and acting in a quasi-governmental role. Fort Vancouver, established by HBC in 1825, was the primary headquarters in the western region and a major trading post until the headquarters moved to the sheltered harbour of Fort Victoria in 1846, at the south end of Vancouver Island, where the first legislature was established a few years later.[11]

Douglas, as Chief Factor, was in a position of considerable power in the colonies before taking on official government duties on November 19, 1858. Douglas became Governor of the Crown Colonies of Vancouver Island and British Columbia, overseeing

---

9 The term at the time referred to someone of mixed-race ancestry who was not a slave. "James Douglas was born in Demerara, British Guiana, which is now Guyana, in 1803. His father was a Scottish merchant with commercial interests in sugar plantations, his mother was a free woman of Barbadian-Creole ancestry." *Earliest Pioneers (1858–1899), Sir James Douglas, Stories, BC Black History Awareness Society.* https://bcblackhistory.ca/sir-james-douglas/

10 *Sir James Douglas,* The Canadian Encyclopedia, April 29, 2022. https://www.thecanadianencyclopedia.ca/en/article/sir-james-douglas

11 *Hudson's Bay Company*, HBC Heritage, 2016. https://www.hbcheritage.ca/classroom/timeline

some of the wild gold rush days and early land and resource agreements. The lure of gold and rich resources defined a passion for the wilderness of British Columbia that carved out a lasting legacy in terms of names and infrastructure, setting the foundation of political power that lasted for decades. Douglas' strong personality ensured that his name would be remembered in the development of the government institutions later.

Douglas' leadership was replaced in 1864 by Arthur Edward Kennedy, who served until 1871, and then British Columbia had our first official premier, John Foster McCreight. A University of British Columbia analysis of the first BC premier, written in 1947, recognizes that personality played a role in political legacy from the beginning.

> John Foster McCreight is not well known in the story of British Columbia, yet he held two of the highest offices— that of Premier and Judge of the Supreme Court... He was of a retiring disposition, more concerned with the formation of statutes and correct legal interpretation than with more popular matters. He was not a man of his times because he stood for learning and principle in a period when action and expediency were more evident. His memory is over- shadowed by that of Amor De Cosmos and Judge Begbie, both of whom were more vivid personalities.[12]

The second premier of British Columbia was named Amor de Cosmos, which means "lover of the universe." Born as William Alexander Smith in 1825 in Nova Scotia, he was from a Loyalist family. He moved to California in 1852 to seek his fortune in the California goldfields. When he arrived, he set himself up as a

12 *John Foster McCreight: first premier of British Columbia*, Patricia Mary Johnson, University of British Columbia, 1947, https://open.library.ubc.ca/soa/cIRcle/collections/ubctheses/831/items/1.0107082

photographer instead, and reinvented himself, changing his name to Amor de Cosmos through the passing of a bill in the California Senate in 1854.[13] Many followers of politics in British Columbia know the name of Amor de Cosmos, although few realize he was the second premier.

De Cosmos headed north in 1858 in pursuit of gold, and almost immediately founded *The British Colonist* newspaper in Victoria. The paper had a mandate to examine all issues of public interest, especially in terms of governance. It was not an objective news source, and it had an activist tone to most stories. *The British Colonist* became a public platform to publish de Cosmos' critical views of what was portrayed as the elitist rule of Governor James Douglas, and the overreaching powers of the Hudson Bay Company. The publication was launched in the midst of the gold rush and before the two Crown colonies joined the confederation of Canada. All of the issues of this paper are published online as of the writing of this book. After a merger with another publication, the newspaper evolved into *The Victoria Times-Colonist*, which continues daily news coverage, and has a representative in the Press Gallery providing a specific focus on the legislative assembly in BC's capital city.[14]

De Cosmos was a strong advocate for democracy, and his published opinions led him to a political career. He held office on and off from 1863 until 1882, including in the legislative assembly of Victoria, the House of Commons, and as premier from 1872 to 1874. Although he had a relatively short time as premier, his legacy was considerable from his work before, during, and after. He is known as the loudest voice in favour of bringing British Columbia into the confederation of Canada. He was a passionate

---

13 *Amor de Cosmos, The Canadian Encyclopedia*, October 28, 2015.
    https://www.thecanadianencyclopedia.ca/en/article/amor-de-cosmos
14 *The British Colonist* (online edition), University of Victoria
    libraries, 1858–1980.

populist, following up on McCreight's policies to initiate a public school system, reduce bureaucracy, extend property rights for married women, and the implement a secret ballot.[15] He was an advocate of equal rights, social justice, and opportunities for all, a true populist for his times.

The first general priorities of the early premiers of BC helped set the tone for later governments: equality, respect, democracy, and progressive policies which would be discussed by elected officials even as economic opportunities were offered by the abundance of the land and the climate of community.

All of these progressive policies were in the context of the times, however, so there were also very popular laws and loud opinions that institutionalized racism against East Asians, South Asians, and Indigenous people, and women were treated as legally inferior in terms of voting and economic independence.

Figure 2: Premier Amor de Cosmos pushing a Chinese worker as part of the overt oppression culture of the times, 1858

With a premier who was so outspoken, popular, and progressive for his time, how did the premiership for de Cosmos end? His is the first of many high-profile and career-ending resignations because of scandal and allegations of corruption.

De Cosmos was forced to resign when there were allegations that he had private interests connected to a major government initiative he was advocating for regional economic development. His political opponents rallied a mob, stormed the legislature, and created considerable noise and

---

15   *Amor de Cosmos, The Canadian Encyclopedia*, Ibid.

confusion around his project for a dry dock in Esquimalt that had received a federal funding commitment after considerable lobbying by de Cosmos.

De Cosmos resigned as the legislative representative for Victoria and faced charges of extortion and corruption. His career was over, and he was effectively silenced because his public image was so damaged by the allegations. He was later cleared of these charges by a BC royal commission, although the clearing was not as high-profile and the damage had been done to his public image.[16]

The cycle, tone, and outcomes of BC's political origins as described above set the stage for a dramatic progression of high-profile players, and literally inspired theatre. In "Shedding the Colonial Past: Rethinking British Columbia Theatre" author James Hoffman quotes University of Victoria professor Terry Morley as saying "politics in British Columbia is theatre and the legislative buildings furnish the locale for the main stage".[17] Hoffman adds, "Surely for theatre we need look only at the province itself, at the spectacle of its 'super/natural' scenery, the plotlines for its melodramatic history, and, especially, the saints and shysters of its wily dramatis personae..."[18]

The blurred line between private media and government continued for over one hundred years, as did the pattern of allegations of corruption against political leaders, followed by resignations and a change in political leadership. With the advent of social and online media in the late 1900s and early 2000s, there is more transparency in the agenda of the publications; however, the focus of stories tends to be the controversy rather than the outcome

16 *De Cosmos, Amor, Volume XII (1891–1900)*, DCB/DBC Mobile beta, Biographi.ca. http://www.biographi.ca/en/bio/de_cosmos_amor_12E. html

17 *Shedding the Colonial Past: Rethinking British Columbia Theatre*, James Hoffman, *The British Columbia Quarterly*, No. 137, Spring 2003. https://ojs.library.ubc.ca/index.php/bcstudies/article/view/1658

18 *Shedding the Colonial Past*, ibid.

of any objective review, such as a commission or investigation. Since this dynamic of scandal/resignation/change of power began in British Columbia, there have been investigations of the claims. Most of the allegations are cleared later, but this has no impact on the change in political leadership because this happens years later and by then, no one in power has any stake in talking about it. Therefore the actual results of the investigation are seldom reported, and frequently the public is left with the impression that the allegations were true, even if they are later disproven by an objective process.

Chapter 3
FREE ENTERPRISE POLITICS

*Agriculture, manufactures, commerce, and navigation, the
four pillars of our prosperity, are the most thriving when left
most free to individual enterprise.*

—Thomas Jefferson[19]

A succession of premiers from 1874 until 1903 ruled British
Columbia independent of party politics, as the province continued to grow its resource economy, secure its relationship relative
to the United States, and try to determine its best relationship
with Ottawa. In 1903, after many years of political party evolution
involving Liberals and Conservatives, Sir Richard McBride became
the first premier to serve on behalf of a political party.[20] He was
also the first premier to be born in British Columbia, and at 32
years old, he is the youngest premier in BC history as of 2023.[21] He

19   *The Writings of Thomas Jefferson*, Richard Holland Johnston, *Thomas Jefferson
     Memorial Association of the United States.*

20   "Former Premiers of British Columbia," CanadaInfo, December 4,
     2022. https://www.craigmarlatt.com/canada/provinces&territories/
     BC_premiers.html

21   *The Politics of Richard McBride*, Course Hero, UBC.
     https://www.coursehero.com/file/p4ok4p69/The-Politics-of-Richard-
     McBride-Sir-Richard-McBride-was-both-the-first-BC-born/

served as a Conservative premier, although his initial partisan label was "Liberal–Conservative."[22] So even at this stage, there was some form of collaboration between two parties that were federal antagonists, a type of foreshadowing of what would emerge decades later.

With a BC premier representing a political party, a new dynamic with the federal government was created, wherein the tension between the province and Ottawa was redefined to include party politics. McBride vocally opposed federal policies advocated by the Liberal government in Ottawa and worked with the federal Conservatives to advance BC's interest and elect Conservative MPs. McBride was elected to the legislature before becoming premier, and served as premier from 1903 until 1915, weathering several controversies and endorsing anti-Asian and anti-Indigenous policies. The voters were white men, while Asians and Indigenous people had no vote, so these policies were popular.

McBride helped to open up many parts of the province with railways and rural infrastructure, paying off provincial debt and raising funds through bonds. He was very protective of British Columbia and concerned about the province's vulnerability to attacks from enemies via the ocean, given BC's relative isolation from federal defense resources. When war broke out in Europe in 1914, he advanced over $1 million of provincial funding to acquire two submarines to protect the coast, quickly transferring them at cost to the federal government. Little did he know that his passion to protect his province would contain the seeds of his political downfall.

The submarines were built in Seattle and meant for Chile. When Chile did not pay for them, McBride stepped in to buy them and was loudly criticized. Only much later was his decision reconsidered in certain circles.

---

22 *Sir Richard McBride, Dictionary of Canadian Biography, Volume XIV (1911–1920).* http://www.biographi.ca/en/bio/mcbride_richard_14E.html

McBride has often been the butt of jokes about zany B.C. politicians, but after the war the official military history concluded his unilateral decision had been a stroke of genius: "The acquisition of these submarines probably saved, as it is believed by many, including high naval authorities, the cities of Victoria and Vancouver, or one or the other of them from attack...What Sir Richard McBride did in those days of great anxiety, even distress, and what he accomplished deserves the commendation of his fellow countrymen."

McKelvie wrote in his memoir that when the German cruisers arrived in the eastern Pacific, it was word that McBride's submarines now patrolled the Strait of Juan de Fuca that provided the most potent deterrent.

Leipzig, unknown to frightened Vancouverites, turned and sped south to rejoin von Spee's squadron at Valparaiso.[23]

Soon after the transfer of the submarines from BC to the federal government, a federal Liberal alleged that money from the transaction had made its way to the Conservative party. A royal commission found that this was not the case, but the exoneration of McBride came years after he had retired.[24]

The best remembered McBride scandal is about the Pacific Great Eastern Railway, a line that McBride advocated as a key part of BC's development, and an additional resource in case of war. McBride tied his political fortune to its completion, and when the construction started to run out of cash, he pushed harder for fast completion. This led to a disaster.

---

23 *Remembrance: When war came close to home*, Stephen Hume, *Vancouver Sun*, November 6, 2014. https://vancouversun.com/news/metro/remembrance-when-war-came-close-to-home

24 Ibid.

> Despite an extra $30,000 cash loan, the railway was on the verge of bankruptcy, and Premier McBride has promised... that the CNR would be completed before (the legislature) reconvened (Regehr, 1976, p.389). Lack of money and time made that promise increasingly difficult to fulfill. McBride responded on one hand by urgently applying for more federal funds, stressing that the alternative line was necessary under conditions of imminent war. On the other hand, he tried to accelerate the pace of construction by demanding that lights be strung in through the canyon so that labourers could work day and night. The premier required that men "[work] double shifts in the canyon..."[25]

These dictates on the pace and method of work are blamed for the accident that happened, which was an enormous landslide at Hell's Gate in the Fraser Canyon. The slide had a disastrous impact on the fisheries, led to serious shortages of food for the Indigenous people, and created political havoc for McBride, halting work on the railway.

The country was soon at war in World War I, and the federal government called in the interest payments on the railway loans. When the BC government had to make a partial payment, the Liberal opposition alleged corruption and kickbacks, a scandal that followed the Conservatives into the election. McBride resigned as premier in December 1915.

In the decades that followed the introduction of Liberal and Conservative parties to BC politics, there would be many similar patterns of populist leaders whose ideas captured voters, helped to build the province, and then became part of the narrative leading to a controversy and scandal ending their reign. It is in the context

---

25 *Constructing and Deconstructing the Railway through Reserves in British Columbia*, Nadine Schuurman, *Native Studies Review* 13, no. 1, 2000, University of Saskatchewan, pp. 19 to 39.

of these patterns that we find people like Rich Coleman who work both in the background and in the public eye to ensure that government continues to govern, and who speak on behalf of the government to support the government and leader's agenda. As British Columbia continued to evolve and grow, the workers became more vocal and began to organize politically. The pattern of scandal as a tool to destabilize political parties and wrestle for power carried through to the labour movement.

Chapter 4
THE LABOUR MOVEMENT

*WE AIM TO REPLACE the present capitalist system,
with its inherent injustice and inhumanity, by a social order
from which the domination and exploitation of one class by
another will be eliminated, in which economic planning will
supersede unregulated private enterprise and competition,
and in which genuine democratic self-government, based
upon economic equality will be possible. The present order
is marked by glaring inequalities of wealth and opportunity,
by chaotic waste and instability; and in an age of plenty
it condemns the great mass of the people to poverty and
insecurity. Power has become more and more concentrated
into the hands of a small irresponsible minority of financiers
and industrialists and to their predatory interests the
majority are habitually sacrificed ... We believe that these
evils can be removed only in a planned and socialized
economy in which our natural resources and principal means
of production and distribution are owned, controlled and
operated by the people.*

—The Regina Manifesto, 1933

From 1871 until 1903, premiers were elected without political affiliation. After 1903, political parties played a pivotal role
in elections. Conservative and Liberal leaders took turns in

government—McBride held the post from 1903 to 1915, his Conservative successor to 1916, and then a series of Liberal premiers were in power from 1916 until 1952, with the exception of five years from 1928 to 1933 when Simon Fraser Tolmie led the Conservatives. These were all pro-business governments, with labourers shut out of decision-making and forced to be heard through public protests or publications.

During these decades, workers, farmers, and others began seeking an expansion of rights for those outside the elites, and movements toward organizing labour started in 1906. These efforts were happening across Canada, with participants in British Columbia. Who would decide how far these organizations would go between advocacy and political representation? How extreme was the ideology? Was it about workers' rights or political power? This was a source of debate.

Early efforts to create a political organization out of the Trades and Labour Congress were opposed by those wanting to create a Socialist Party, and because of this argument, neither of these groups succeeded in creating a formal organization. It was in 1921 that the Communist Party of Canada was formed;[26] however, this did not appear to have any real impact on the political success of the Conservatives and the Liberals in BC. It was only with the creation of the Co-operative Commonwealth Federation (CCF) in 1932 that the two main political parties finally faced a serious challenge from an opposing ideology that represented people outside of the business classes.

The CCF was founded in Calgary in 1932 during the Great Depression, and it brought together people from farmers' movements, socialist groups, and labour activism, finally providing a cohesive forum for their advocacy. There were member organizations in each province across Canada, providing an immediate

26 *The development of the CCF*, Ross Dowson, March 13, 2006.
https://www.marxists.org/archive/dowson/speeches/rdspeechLP2.html

national and regional membership and supporter base.[27] The motivation to create the CCF followed the stock market crash of 1929 and a lengthy drought that impacted farmers and hurt the economy. The need for a national political movement representing workers emerged because Liberal Prime Minister Mackenzie King and Conservative Opposition Leader RB Bennett stated there was no need for extraordinary measures to address the problems. The provincial governments were left to respond to the social problems caused by the economic hardship.[28]

The Regina Manifesto was created in 1933 and stated the core principles of the CCF, taking direct aim at the Liberal and Conservative parties:

> This social and economic transformation can be brought about by political action, through the election of a government inspired by the ideal of a Co-operative Commonwealth and supported by a majority of the people. We do not believe in change by violence. We consider that both the old parties in Canada are the instruments of capitalist interests and cannot serve as agents of social reconstruction, and that whatever the superficial differences between them, they are bound to carry on government in accordance with the dictates of the big business interests who finance them. The CCF aims at political power in order to put an end to this capitalist domination of our political life. It is a democratic movement, a federation of

---

27 *The Impact of the C.C.F. on Canadian Parties and Groups*, Dean McHenry, *The Journal of Politics*, University of Chicago Press, Vol. 11, No. 2, May 1949=. https://www.jstor.org/stable/2126282

28 *Rise of the Co-operative Commonwealth Federation*, Laura Neilson Bonikowsky, *The Canadian Encyclopedia*, March 4, 2015. https://www.thecanadianencyclopedia.ca/en/article/tommy-douglas-greatest-canadian-feature

farmer, labour and socialist organizations, financed by its own members and seeking to achieve its ends solely by constitutional methods.[29]

This manifesto changed the public conversation about the role of government because it provided promises of unemployment and health insurance plans, public housing, agricultural price supports, farm financing, and public ownership of major institutions, including financial institutions. This changed the landscape of public advocacy across the country at a time when people were looking for leadership and hope that with sound strategies, the people could rebuild the economy and create long-term plans for the future.

In addition, this party created an enormous change in attitude toward people of colour. Previously, white male leaders were able to recruit political support by appealing to the only demographic who could vote: white men. Now, white male leadership was speaking to the issue of non-white non-voters and advocating a different approach.

Under the leadership of J.S. Woodsworth, who was a devout Christian, this new political party began the first conversations about treating immigrants with respect, rather than as commodities and cheap labour. By the time Woodsworth became leader of the CCF, he had been elected as a Member of Parliament for Winnipeg for 12 years. His tireless work on behalf of the disadvantaged led to Canada's first social welfare legislation in 1926, when he provided enough votes to keep Mackenzie King in power in

---

29   *The CCF's Regina Manifesto*, Co-operative Commonwealth Federation, *The Canadian Dimension*, May 7, 2018. https://canadiandimension.com/ articles/view/the-regina-manifesto-1933-co-operative-commonwealth-federation-programme-fu

exchange for the introduction of an old age pension plan.[30]

The Regina Manifesto's ideas took hold quickly in British Columbia. In 1933, BC made history by becoming the first full battleground for the CCF, when the CCF fought the general election in BC with a full slate of candidates. To be able to run a full slate of candidates the same year that the Regina Manifesto was published was a clear indication of how receptive the workers of British Columbia were to these policies.

Share of seats in the British Columbia legislature at general elections, 1871-2017

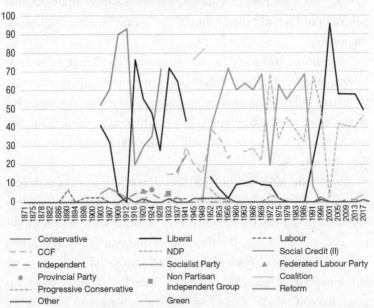

Figure 3: Popular Vote in BC General Elections, from Molineaux, ibid.

30 *Making Medicare, the History of Health Care in Canada, 1914–1929, J.S. Woodsworth*, Canadian Museum of History, Musee Canadien de l'Histoire. https://www.historymuseum.ca/cmc/exhibitions/hist/medicare/medic-1k10e.html

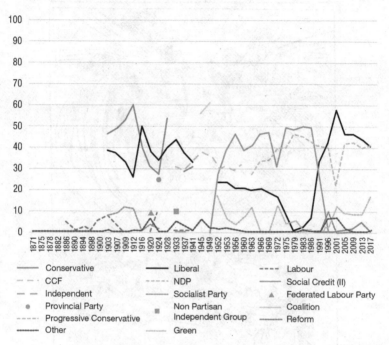

Share of popular vote in British Columbia
general elections, 1871-2017

——— Conservative	——— Liberal
— — · CCF	······· NDP
— — Independent	——— Socialist Party
● Provincial Party	■ Non Partisan
····· Progressive Conservative	Independent Group
——— Other	——— Green

---- Labour
——— Social Credit (II)
▲ Federated Labour Party
——— Coalition
——— Reform

**Figure 4: Share of Seats in BC elections,
from Molineaux, ibid**

The political rhetoric and media coverage of the 1933 election was extreme, marking it as a fight for the future of capitalism between the business parties and the CCF, capitalism versus socialism.

Figure 5: Vancouver Sun illustration of the fight
between the CCF and Liberals, 1933

Going into the election battle, the Conservatives were in government under the leadership of Simon Fraser Tolmie. Tolmie was a veterinarian and a farmer, and he had previously served as a Member of Parliament for the Unionist Party. In 1926 he left federal politics to become Leader of the Conservative Party of BC and was elected as MLA in Saanich and became premier in 1928. His government faced the challenges of the Great Depression. Civil unrest in the wake of the Depression and unhappiness with the federal Conservative government led to internal fighting in the BC Conservatives.[31] Tolmie left the Conservative party before the 1933 election and ran for re-election with the support of Unionist Party members. This change and the internal weakness of his new political party rendered his party irrelevant. This meant the election was a fight between the Liberals and the CCF.

The comments from Liberal Leader Thomas Dufferin (Duff) Pattullo at that time set the tone for decades to come, when he called on all non-socialists and asked them not to split the vote, because doing so could result in political chaos. In a rallying speech at the Hotel Vancouver on October 23, 1933, Pattullo said:

> "I appeal to people of all shades of political opinion, Conservative, Liberal and those of more radical trends, to save the good name of British Columbia by rallying behind the only instrument through which stable and progressive government can be maintained in this province."

Extreme claims set the tone; the capitalist side was at war with the socialists. The Liberals attacked William Pritchard, leader of the CCF, as a criminal because he had served jail time for participating in the Winnipeg General Strike in 1919. The Liberals claimed the goal of the CCF was to enact radical change, and in a meeting at the Hotel Vancouver one week after Pattullo's speech Gerry McGeer, later to be Mayor of Vancouver, claimed that if the CCF won the election, "it [would mean] revolution. The Dominion (of Canada) would declare war and take charge of British Columbia, and we would lose all our personal freedom."[32]

---

31 *Simon Fraser Tolmie*, Dr. Patricia E. Roy, *The Canadian Encyclopedia*, December 15, 2013. https://www.thecanadianencyclopedia.ca/en/article/simon-fraser-tolmie

32 *This Week in History, 1933: The CCF fights its first full election in British Columbia*, John Mackie, *Vancouver Sun*, October 30, 2020. https://vancouversun.com/news/politics/this-week-in-history-1933-the-ccf-fights-its-first-full-election-in-british-columbia

The Liberals went after Pritchard with personal attacks, and many extreme claims were made about the potential tragedies of voting for the CCF. The scare tactics employed by the Liberals were effective in delivering them power. In the election of November 2, 1933, the Liberals won a landslide of 34 seats with almost 42% of the vote, while the brand new CCF took almost 32% of the vote, winning only 7 seats, and the Unionists took 4% of the vote, electing one person. Tolmie himself was defeated.

Premier Duff Pattullo was definitely a larger-than-life leader, known for his elegant style and London fashions. Driven, aggressive, and often prone to acting in the grey area of administrative rules to get his agenda accomplished, Pattullo had a restless energy that baffled the politicians from rural farm backgrounds, like his Conservative predecessor Simon Fraser Tolmie. According to the analysis by Charles L. Shaw printed in *Maclean's* on January 1, 1934:

(Pattullo) knew that government in these days is no bed of roses, no pleasant sinecure. Probably he realized, as many others did, that the voters had not really wanted Pattullo so much as they had wanted a stable government—a change from the vacillating policy of the latter days of the Tolmie régime, and a sure bulwark against the rise of the Co-operative Commonwealth Federation, the big, bad wolf of 1933 politics in British Columbia. Thousands of lifelong Tories voted Liberal not because they liked the Liberals more but because they liked the C. C. F. and its promise of radical legislation less, and because the Conservatives were so thoroughly split and subdivided that a vote for them would be useless.[33]

---

33 Pattullo of B.C.: *He used to startle Yukon miners with his white flannels—He's B.C.'s most elegant premier and he landslid the Tories out*, Charles Shaw, *Maclean's* Magazine, January 1, 1934. https://archive.macleans.ca/article/1934/1/1/pattullo-of-b-c

His personality traits included fearless determination and an ability to overcome criticism in his relentless pursuit of his goals. First elected in 1916, he had considerable experience in government and opposition before he took over as premier. Previous experience in land speculation gave him knowledge of business, and he also had a reputation for efficiency in executing decisions. Decisiveness in leadership in BC has been generally rewarded by the voters.

Pattullo's slogan in the 1933 election was "Work and Wages" and his key quote defining his government's attitude was: "We are living in one of the greatest evolutionary periods in human history... Where precedent is good we are going to follow it. Where precedent is bad we will ignore it. And where it is necessary to create precedent we will create it."[34]

From the time of Pattullo's election in 1933 until the general election of 1952, the Liberal Party held power in British Columbia. Pattullo ruled until 1941 and was succeeded by John Hart, who led the province from 1941 to 1947, and who was succeeded by Byron Ingemar Johnson, who led from 1947 to 1952. This was a time of relative quiet on the capitalist side, in the wake of the confusion between Unionist and Conservative voters and the strength of the Liberals. The overall power structure in BC's political landscape continued to shift during these years with each subsequent Liberal victory, and the response to this shift provided an opening for populist change.

Regardless of the outcome of the election, the fact that the CCF had elected representatives and taken almost one-third of the vote in their first election changed politics in British Columbia permanently, entrenching the tension between the capitalist and worker ideologies and the fight for power over the "commonwealth," which in BC is the resource base. The vast wealth of the province fed the economy and created jobs. The tension between

---

34   *Pattullo of B.C.*, ibid.

business and labour grew with the expansion of the economy and the increased stakes over who controlled the levers of power.

Why did the CCF continue to grow in popularity when the capitalist representatives predicted such dire consequences? CCF Leader William Pritchard was a passionate and idealistic orator, committed to fighting for social justice and standing up for his convictions with respect to workers' rights. A compelling speaker, editor of *The Western Clarion*, and an early member of the Socialist Party, Pritchard was fearless in his commentary, including publicly stating his opinion that labour activist Ginger Goodwin had been murdered by the special constable in Cumberland—a statement Pritchard made publicly more than once after examining Goodwin's body directly.[35]

Pritchard's convictions and strong principles inspired generations of socialist leaders, and decades later his grandson Bob Williams would emerge as a giant in public policy in government, with the ideas from the 1930s continuing to resonate and drive projects when the NDP formed government in the 1970s, and later, when Williams re-entered the private sector as a policy leader in the credit unions.

Strong opinions guided Pattullo in his pursuit of a better British Columbia. He is best known today for the Pattullo Bridge, a major infrastructure project that crossed the Fraser River at New Westminster. Built in only one year, it cost $4 million in 1936 dollars and was considered a masterpiece of engineering.[36]

Pattullo is remembered for his advocacy of "socialized credit," his public works that led to jobs in BC, and his fights with Ottawa over financial policies.

---

35 *William Pritchard and Paying a Price for the Winnipeg General Strike*, Rod Mickleburgh, *Mickleblog*, June 21, 2019. https://mickleblog.wordpress. com/2019/06/21/william-pritchard-and-paying-a-price-for-the-winnipeg-general-strike/

36 *This Week in History: Premier Thomas Dufferin Pattullo*, Veronica Cooper, *CHEK News*, September 8, 2018. https://www.cheknews.ca/ this-week-in-history-premier-thomas-dufferin-pattullo-485274/

A man of his times, Pattullo was also openly racist and exploi-
tive of Asian workers. He tried to intervene with the federal
government's efforts to have Chinese-Canadian recruits in the
Second World War, attempting to block them so that they would
have a harder time obtaining citizenship. He wrote to the prime
minister saying that people who were born in Canada and were
of Chinese ancestry should not be allowed to serve in the war,
because the service would undermine the justification for denying
them equal rights. These policies led to calls in 2020 to rename
the Pattullo Bridge.[37]

When Pattullo sought his third mandate in 1941, he won a
minority government of 21 seats out of the 48-seat legislature,
and the Conservatives rebuilt to 12 seats. It was a time of war. The
CCF had increased their representation in the legislature to 14
seats, and Independent Labour had 1 seat.

The non-socialist political forces called loudly for a new align-
ment, a coalition of Liberals and Conservatives. Pattullo fought
it with the same drive he had shown for decades, stating with
surprising insight that if the Liberals entered a coalition with the
Conservatives, the Liberal Party "will start downhill, and never
again within a generation will it be the power it has been in
British Columbia. In a year or two at most, it will be forced to go
to the people as a union party."[38]

Pattullo lost the battle against the coalition and was removed
from a leadership position by a combination of Liberals and
Conservatives led by John Hart, a Liberal who became the next
premier. He was defeated in his bid for re-election in 1945 and

---

37 *Calls to stop Honouring 'racist' former premier by taking name off new Pattullo
    Bridge,* Jon Woodward, *CTV News,* October 8, 2020.
    https://bc.ctvnews.ca/calls-to-stop-honouring-racist-former-premier-by-
    taking-name-off-new-pattullo-bridge-1.5137383
38 Duff Pattullo and the Coalition Controversy of 1941, George M. Abbott,
    BC Studies, No. 102, Summer 1994.

retired from politics.[39]

After its first foray into formal politics in the 1933 election, the CCF continued to build strength and attract support, refining its message and organization, both nationally and in British Columbia. CCF members and candidates spoke repeatedly before, during, and after elections, articulating ideas for social programs including universal health care, public pensions, workers' rights, and labour laws to protect workers from exploitation. The work of the CCF motivated governments to implement new programs.

(Prime Minister Mackenzie) King and his party responded to the CCF's success by adopting some of the party's most popular policies, cutting off the threat on the left and initiating the federal government's involvement in social and economic affairs. The Liberals hoped to prevent a post-war Depression and in the process laid the foundation for Canada's welfare state. To the Old Age Pension plan, they added an unemployment-insurance scheme (1940) and a system of family allowances (1944). They also promoted policies to support home building, find work for demobilized war vets and increase federal assistance to health care.[40]

While the policies and programs advocated by the CCF resonated with people across Canada, World War II provided the powerful opponents of the CCF with an opportunity to describe the CCF as communists, linking them to the Soviet Union and fascist dictatorships, playing on the fears and raw emotions of the

39 *Pattullo, Thomas Dufferin, 1873-1956, BC Archives Collection Search*, Royal BC Museum, 1975. https://search.bcarchives.gov.bc.ca/pattullo-thomas-dufferin-1873-1956

40 *Rise of the Co-operative Commonwealth Federation*, Laura Neilson Bonikowsky, *the Canadian Encyclopedia*, March 4, 2015. https://www.thecanadianencyclopedia.ca/en/article/tommy-douglas-greatest-canadian-feature

electorate in the post-war era. Although the CCF was opposed to communism and advocated socialism through democratic elections, the uniform and high-profile messages of their opponents caused a lot of damage to the CCF's ability to be seen for their policy positions.[41]

Since the origin of the CCF (which became the NDP), there has rarely been a situation where the labour party has less than 25% of the voting base as its foundational support. Sometimes, the percentage is much higher. With the exception of the 2001 election, when the popular vote for the NDP dipped to 21.6%, the CCF/NDP support has been between 30 and 40%.[42] Political success was dependent on how the popular vote was distributed amongst ridings throughout the province, and on whether the Liberals and Conservatives were collaborating, whether directly or through a coalition political party such as the Social Credit Party, or the BC Liberal Party, after 1994.

41 *Canada's first socialist party emerges from the prairie Dust Bowl*, Co-operative Commonwealth Federation, *Le Canada, A People's History*, CBC Learning, 2001. https://www.cbc.ca/history/EPISCONTENTSE1EP13CH3 PA1LE.html

42 *Contagion in the West: The Survival and Success of the CCF-NDP in Western Canada*, Connor John Molineaux, University of Calgary, *PRISM Repository*, The Vault, April 30, 2021, pp. 130–138.

Chapter 5
THE SOCIAL CREDIT DYNASTY

For in a democracy, every citizen, regardless of his interest in politics, "hold office"; every one of us is in a position of responsibility; and, in the final analysis, the kind of government we get depends upon how we fulfill those responsibilities. We, the people, are the boss, and we will get the kind of political leadership, be it good or bad, that we demand and deserve.

—John F. Kennedy[43]

Meanwhile, a populist movement began in British Columbia to respond to the dissatisfaction of some voters who did not appreciate the Liberal/Conservative coalition. It began in Alberta with the new Social Credit Party, which had an ideology that economic challenges were caused because the money supply was inadequate. A radio evangelist named William Aberhart was the first high-profile proponent of Social Credit, and he claimed that the Great Depression would have been avoided if the banks printed more money and supplied it to consumers, whose expenditures would stimulate the economy. Social Credit was elected to government

---

43   Kennedy, John F, from "Profiles in Courage." www.jfklibrary.org, 1957

in 1935[44], and a Social Credit political party began in BC around the same time; however, it did not gain any significant support until a series of circumstances opened the door to a new political dynasty.

In 1952, British Columbia's political landscape changed dramatically. There were several key factors:

- first, the loose loyalty that Liberal and Conservative voters had to the governing coalition;

- second, the ongoing and loud rhetoric characterizing the CCF as a huge threat to democracy and freedom, even as the CCF was gaining popularity;

- third, a Conservative MLA named William Andrew Cecil Bennett, elected out of Kelowna in the interior of BC, who, having failed in two bids to lead the Conservative party, left the Conservative caucus to sit as an independent in the Victoria legislature; [45]

- fourth, the Social Credit Party's slate of candidates for the 1952 election, of which Bennett was one; and finally,

- fifth, the Liberal/Conservative coalition, concerned about the rising influence of the CCF and the potential of losing power, set up a unique alternative voting system to try to ensure that one of their parties would win government.

As the saying goes, the best laid plans of mice and men often go awry... The alternative vote was the key factor in ensuring that the coalition lost power to a new party. As H.F. Angus explains:

---

44 Social Credit Party of Canada, Oxford Reference, 2023.
    https://www.oxfordreference.com/display/10.1093/oi/authority.2011080
    3100515461;jsessionid=7E4AD8413F4FF1560D99BA64EB1655F9

45 *W.A.C. Bennett*, Patricia E. Roy and Danny Kucharsky, *The Canadian Encyclopedia*, January 30, 2018. https://www.thecanadianencyclopedia.ca/en/article/william-andrew-cecil-bennett

Although the Coalition had been dissolved and the Conservatives became the official Opposition, the Liberals and Conservatives were still conscious of a certain community of interest. Indeed, an ingenious attempt was made to continue, by the introduction of a system of alternative voting... At the election of 1949 the C.C.F. party had obtained 35.1 percent of the votes, comprising those of convinced socialists and those of malcontents... it seemed not improbable that, in a three-cornered contest, the C.C.F. might secure a majority of the 48 seats and find itself in a position to make drastic changes in the economic institutions of the province... by using the alternative vote the electors could give their first choice to a Liberal and their second choice to a Conservative, and vice versa, and so confine the C.C.F. to those constituencies in which it enjoyed an absolute majority.[46]

The assumptions by the Liberals and Conservatives that the voters would choose one in first position and one in second position completely overlooked the deep-seated antagonism of true Conservatives for true Liberals, and vice versa, plus the fact that there was a third, and emerging, capitalist political party. The unusual voting system led to an enormous amount of confusion after the election, and it took some time to declare Social Credit as the party with the highest number of elected members. The outcome that delivered government to the Social Credit Party is almost certainly one that could only happen in British Columbia as an ongoing part of the random politics. Canada's national magazine *Maclean's* had a lot of fun describing the representatives of the new government.

---

46   *Notes and Memoranda, the British Columbia Election, June, 1952*, H. F. Angus, *The Canadian Journal of Economics and Political Science*, Vol. 18, No. 4, November 1952. https://www.jstor.org/stable/138370

The party went to the polls with no leader. Not until after the election did Social Credit's nineteen elected MLAs and its defeated candidates get around to choosing a premier-elect. The party did not have a lawyer on its slate but it elected three preachers for the first time in B. C. provincial history, and otherwise was well represented with school-teachers, general-store keepers, farmers, a Boy Scout leader, a shoe repair man, a hog grader, a railroad engineer and a naturopathic physician.

The party's provincial president, who shared the national Social Credit ambition to take over the Bank of Canada, had never brushed closer to high finance than the coin box of the Vancouver trolley bus on which he was a driver.[47]

BC political commentator Will McMartin provided a contemporary analysis in a regional publication. Entitled *BC Then, Ottawa Now: Who's Crazier?* He wrote in 2008 that "if ever an unusual or bizarre parliamentary event has occurred anywhere in history, it probably did so in B.C." McMartin provides a perspective on the events leading up to the advent of the Social Credit dynasty in BC. Note that the CCF actually won considerably more votes yet lost the election. In 1996, the BC Liberals would experience this in contesting an election they expected to win against the NDP.

A decade later, the coalition's disintegration led to another general election. The results of the 1952 contest were difficult to ascertain: Social Credit, a party that never before had elected an MLA in B.C., led the way with 19, and close behind (despite taking 28,000 more votes than the Socreds) was the CCF with 18 seats.

---

47   *How Social Credit Took BC*, various authors, *Maclean's*, September 1, 1952.

The Liberals returned six MLAs and the Conservatives had four. Tom Uphill, the veteran Independent, also won re-election.

Clarence Wallace, B.C.'s lieutenant governor, seemed as confused by the results as most British Columbians. He delayed and dithered for nearly a month before W.A.C. Bennett, the Socred leader, insisted on having a meeting. He went to Wallace with a letter from Uphill, who, despite being affiliated with organized labour, evidently had pledged his support to the Socreds and not the CCF.

With Uphill's support, the Socreds could appoint a Speaker and still enjoy a one-seat plurality in the legislative assembly. Wallace capitulated, swearing Bennett and his chosen Social Credit colleagues into the executive council.[48]

This pivotal decision changed the course of BC's history. The Bennett dynasty of Social Credit started with this new government. W.A.C. Bennett's leadership provided massive infrastructure projects that continue to benefit British Columbians well into the twenty-first century, although many of them provide ongoing controversy. A populist leader with a strong vision and rigid opinions, W.A.C. Bennett lived in Kelowna, in the interior of British Columbia, in the Okanagan Valley. His government's perspective was heavily influenced by the reality of the massive size and wealth of the province, and the need to ensure that people and goods could move around relatively easily. Bennett's government created Crown Corporations including BC Hydro and the BC

48   BC Then, Ottawa Now: Who's Crazier? Province's wild political history offers context for current crisis, Will McMartin, The Tyee, Vancouver, BC, December 5, 2008. https://thetyee.ca/News/2008/12/05/BCThenOttawaNow/print.html

Ferry system, and opened up the interior of the province with transportation infrastructure of roads, railways, and bridges at an unprecedented rate.

The strength of the CCF in this same election alarmed the capitalist parties, and attacks on that party's "true" agenda continued, with a particular emphasis on tying it to a frightening vision of the Soviet Union and communism.

Although the CCF was well established, it gradually declined in popular appeal after the war. A democratic socialist party, it was accused of being associated with communism. (See Communist Party of Canada.) During Cold War tensions, this image was damaging. An attempt was made in 1956 to soften the party's image. The Regina Manifesto was replaced with a new, moderate document; the Winnipeg Declaration. However, this could not reverse the trend. In 1958, the party suffered a disastrous defeat; only eight MPs were elected with a mere 9.5 per cent of the popular vote. Both Coldwell and Deputy Leader Stanley Knowles were defeated in their ridings. (See Elections of 1957 and 1958.)[49]

The politically astute organizers of the CCF were firmly committed to continuing the growth in strength of the organization's ideas, even as they recognized that there was little hope of political success if they remained in the CCF, which was branded as communist. Enter national leader David Lewis, who brokered a deal connecting the Canadian Labour Congress with a new political party.

---

49 *Co-operative Commonwealth Federation (CCF)*, J. T. Morley, Julie Smyth, and Andrew McIntosh, *The Canadian Encyclopedia*, March 26, 2021. https://www.thecanadianencyclopedia.ca/en/article/co-operative-commonwealth-federation

The CLC was urged by Lewis to save democratic socialism in Canada; it agreed to enter a formal alliance with the CCF to create a new party. In 1961, the CCF entered a new phase. It emerged from a founding convention as the New Democratic Party.[50]

Soon nicknamed Wacky Bennett by his detractors, William Sr. holds the record as the longest-serving premier in BC history at 20 years. W.A.C. Bennett's government was defeated in 1972 by the NDP, led by Dave Barrett. The Barrett government was hounded by its opponents even as his leadership created the Agricultural Land Reserve and the Insurance Corporation of British Columbia. There were loud controversies about each major decision and much suspicion about the NDP government's real agenda.

In those years, there were no fixed election days, and after a series of major public reforms, Barrett yielded to public pressure and called a general election, which he lost to the Social Credit Party, then led by W.A.C. Bennett's successor, his son William Jr.— known as Bill Bennett and, in the custom of BC politics, nick-named "Mini-W.A.C." Bill was not a populist; however, he was driven to serve the people and held the office of premier for 11 years. He drove an overhaul of the public service, instituted fiscal restraint, brought in the SkyTrain system that continues to serve as a fundamental public transit backbone in Vancouver, welcomed the international Expo 86 fair that catalyzed growth for the lower mainland, and led many other public policy initiatives.

Bill Bennett retired from politics in 1986. Later, he was caught up in a scandal where it was alleged that he was involved in insider trading, and a criminal investigation was launched alongside a securities commission investigation of him, his brother, and Herb

---

50   *Co-operative Commonwealth Federation (CCF)*, ibid.

Doman of Doman Industries, a prominent forest sector company. All three were acquitted of the criminal charges fairly quickly[51]; however, less than two years later the BC Securities Commission started a new investigation. It took 11 years for this process to find them guilty.[52] Their appeal of this ruling was unsuccessful.

51   *Marketwatch*, David Baines, *The Vancouver Sun*, Vancouver, BC, December 27, 1989.

52   B.C. *Securities Commission deserves to be commended: [Final Edition], The Vancouver Sun*, Vancouver, BC, October 18, 1999.

Chapter 6
RETURN OF THE BC LIBERAL PARTY

*Voting is as much an emotional act
as it is an intellectual one.*

—Monica Crowley

Winning an election is all about the math, riding by riding.

—Rich Coleman

The strength of the Bennetts' leadership carried the party for most of its dynasty. Months after Bill Bennett retired, the party elected a charismatic leader, a self-made millionaire who became known for his big smile. His wife Lillian was high-profile and set a style for wearing hairbands. Bill (William) Vander Zalm was an outspoken reformer who was set on breaking down the bureaucracy that was bad for business, and his supporters were loyal. He made headlines frequently with his bold statements, including his commentary as a practising Catholic where he made abortion a key focus of public policy debates.

Vander Zalm was a polarizing figure and was forced out of office by scandal after he was found to be in a Conflict of Interest over the sale of his private property, called Fantasy Gardens. It was an investigation he himself initiated. He had been a controversial leader during his entire tenure and had not contested a general election in that position.

He was replaced by Rita Johnston, BC's first female premier. Johnston lost the 1991 election.[53] This loss was the beginning of the end of Social Credit and was the beginning of the "moderate" public policy positions of the NDP.

Under the leadership of former Vancouver mayor Mike Harcourt, the NDP had a decisive victory in 1991, while the governing Social Credit Party was reduced to 7 seats out of the 75 in the legislature.

One of the biggest news stories out of the 1991 election in BC was the return of the party that would become the BC Liberals, when the Liberals went from zero MLAs to 17 on October 17. At that time, it was called the Liberal Party of British Columbia, and it had recently detached itself from the federal Liberal Party. The BC Liberal Party had not elected any MLAs to the legislature since the 1970s, when Gordon Gibson sat as the lone Liberal.[54]

I was one of the MLAs elected that night, under the leadership of Gordon Wilson, a professor of economic geography from Capilano University (then Capilano College) who was also a pig farmer on the Sunshine Coast. Wilson had taken over the leadership of the party by acclamation on October 31, 1987, and had gathered together a tenacious group of supporters who worked hard with him to achieve the breakthrough. His performance in the leaders' debate with Mike Harcourt and Rita Johnston was attributed as the turning point in the election campaign that led to the breakthrough[55].

53   B.C. has first woman premier: [Final Edition], Ken MacQueen, The Windsor Star, Windsor, ON, April 3, 1991.

54   B.C. Liberal Gordon Gibson was a formidable presence in Canada's political life, Andrew Cohen, The Globe and Mail, December 26, 2023.
      https://www.theglobeandmail.com/canada/article-bc-liberal-gordon-gibson-was-a-formidable-presence-in-canadas/

55   Harcourt will be new premier: [First Edition], The Province, Vancouver, BC, October 24, 1991.

At the same time that Wilson was building the Liberals up into a contender, Rich Coleman was in Langley, working hard for the Social Credit Party, trying to help them retain power. We have gone through the origin story of politics and BC, and this has led us to the origin story for Rich Coleman as a key figure for the BC Liberals. This begins in 1991, with his work for the Social Credit Party.

In order to truly understand BC politics, it is really important to understand how different each region is and take into account the significant, and growing, division in perspective between the urban, rural, and remote sections of the province. It's a dynamic that many political parties are ignoring as they focus their policies on the voter-rich urban areas, and the alienation of the other parts of the province is growing.

The most successful leaders in BC have understood the importance of the remote regions as the source of BC's wealth from the primary economy, especially forestry, mining, oil, and gas; the importance of the rural areas in supplying the secondary economy, especially in agriculture; and the importance of the urban areas in managing the tertiary economy. The most successful leaders have been able to weave all three together with policies that resonate across the province, rather than pitting one area against another.

The culture of each region is different. I can provide an oversimplification that gives some context, although to really do justice to the variety would take many more pages. There's the cowboy country of the Cariboo, wine country in the Okanagan, the Bible Belt of the Fraser Valley, the laid-back vibe of the Gulf Islands and Sunshine Coast, the raw energy of Haida Gwaii and the north coast, the rugged independence of the Peace River area, the new age lifestyle of the Kootenays, and the progressively modern lower mainland, where Vancouver rules over the playground and workspaces from the Sea to Sky Highway to the Fraser River.

Each region tends to have its own voting preferences, usually based on party but sometimes driven by regional issues or a response to a government's policies. The Bible Belt and many parts of the interior and north tend to vote for conservative candidates, and the Social Credit Party was conservative. The word "liberal" was a bad word in many places around BC for a long time, the "NDP" much worse in many parts of the interior and north. A representative who spoke to important issues and was a populist would usually transcend party lines, like Bill Barlee did for the NDP in the south Okanagan in 1988, or Dave Zirnhelt in the Cariboo. My surprise election in Kelowna was a result of the split vote and my years of high-profile community engagement on issues like small business, the environment, and agriculture, and was likely helped by my family's strong connection to the wine industry and the Catholic Church. There are many instances where a candidate with a profile similar to mine could win just enough support to be elected, and if he or she did a good job and had strong party support, be re-elected.

The strong and open dislike of the word "liberal" in so many parts of BC contributed to the surprise of many observers when the Liberals went from zero seats to official opposition status. The word itself became problematic for those who yearned for a return of the reins of power but needed a different name for their political party.

Chapter 7
COLEMAN'S EARLY POLITICAL DAYS

I have been involved in volunteer work for over 25 years. I've been a member of fraternal organizations, chambers of commerce, church groups, community groups and service organizations. I recognize how hard the volunteers in the province of British Columbia work to provide for citizens in their community who are less fortunate. From food banks to community services, from children's organizations to handicapped groups, from sports organizations to self-help groups, volunteer and charitable organizations make British Columbia a better place. If you've ever seen the impact of a food hamper at Christmastime, or assisted in relief to those who can't clothe their families, when help arrives—or any other charitable work—you'd be aware of the special relationship that humanity has with itself.

—Rich Coleman, First Speech in
the BC Legislature, July 6, 1996

In the mid-1980s, Rich Coleman ran for council for the municipality of Langley Township twice and lost both times. His friend Bruce Strongitharm was by his side, working hard. Bruce's family had a long history in politics, so he was able to provide a lot of perspective, but it was not enough for the local campaigns. "We had the bright idea that Rich should run for council. We had about $300 and we did terrible. The next time he changed strategy and did better but he still didn't win."

Rich remembers how terrible the local campaigns were. "The first time it was like we didn't know anything. We had cardboard signs, the first rain they got wet, we tried to put plastic on them, it was terrible. I got about 700 votes. Then some people convinced me to run on a slate. It didn't do that well, two of the guys got elected, the other five of us didn't."

His wife, Michele, worked hard. "I cold called the telephone book. I would open up the Aldergrove telephone book and just start phoning people. I didn't have a voters list, I was probably phoning people who couldn't vote. We had crazy cardboard signs and we put saran wrap on them," she still smiles at the memories, "I did it because it was him and he asked me to, I certainly knew he would be good at it if he was elected. I always believed in him."

After this experience, Coleman decided he was not going to run for office again. Through his campaigns he had connected with the Social Credit Party and made a good impression. The SoCreds invited him to be campaign manager in the 1986 election for the MLA in his riding for a candidate named Dan Peterson. It was a success, Petersen was elected, and Coleman experienced the winning side of politics. When Petersen ran for re-election in 1991, Coleman was his campaign manager again. He had a front-row seat when the SoCreds collapsed after the debate performance of BC Liberal Leader Gordon Wilson, and a young candidate named Gary Farrell-Collins (later Gary Collins) defeated the incumbent in a shocking upset.

Coleman remembers the impact. "I was running the phone banks, after that debate the shift was dramatic, the shift happened overnight. It was like everyone was looking for someone who was fresh and honest and Gordon gave them that."

The political landscape of British Columbia changed fundamentally in the 1991 election, with the Social Credit Party dropped from a majority government of 47 out of 69 seats to just 7, while Gordon Wilson's Liberals won a surprising 17 seats, returning the Liberals to the BC legislature for the first time in decades as official opposition. The New Democratic Party under Mike Harcourt won a substantial majority government with 51 of the 75 seats.

I was the only Liberal elected in the interior of the province. I won in the riding of Okanagan East, which represented half of the City of Kelowna. Kelowna was the heartland of Social Credit, home of the Bennetts and a region that was very protective of their power base. In 1991 I defeated Minister of Agriculture Larry Chalmers. I was a pregnant 26-year-old ethnic woman with two small children, an outspoken immigrant from India, and my demographics underscored a dramatic shift for Kelowna in terms of elected representation, since previously all the representatives in senior government had been older white men.

Like Coleman, I had a close view of the collapse of the Social Credit Party and could feel the shock of the long-time Social Credit supporters, who did not know how to respond to a province run by the NDP with the Liberals in opposition and the Social Credit Party reduced to seven relatively obscure MLAs. Most of these people were influential and wealthy or upper middle–income business people.

Coleman was pretty motivated to continue his involvement in provincial politics, especially because he was concerned about the NDP's agenda for BC. Like many British Columbians, he did not support a government run on socialist policies, and he felt displaced as a voter, not sure where his vote and his energy would be best applied. Because of his work in the 1986 and 1991 election campaigns, he was now trained in organization and highly skilled at fundraising and political strategy. The foundation was in place so that he could help a free enterprise party defeat the NDP, but where would he go?

After the 1991 election, there was a lot of confusion amongst SoCred supporters about what they should do before the next election. Many of them did not believe the party was finished. The other Kelowna MLA Cliff Serwa was loyal to the core to Social Credit, ending up as the last Social Credit MLA in 1996. After the 1991 election, the Social Credit Party continued to lose strength.

Four of the MLAs elected as Social Credit banded together to form the BC Reform Party. In order for a political party to have official party status, which provided a higher profile and resources, the minimum number of MLAs was four. In one move, these four MLAs rendered Social Credit defunct in the legislature as it lost official party status and the related funding. The BC Reform Party became the third political party in the legislature, after the NDP and the Liberals. BC Reform Leader Jack Weisgerber, generally respected, was denounced by many loyal Social Credit supporters since they only associated him with the previous governments. He had been a popular and effective cabinet minister in the Social Credit government from 1988 until 1991 and had served as interim leader of the Social Credit Party after the 1991 election.

Between the 1991 and 1996 elections, political operatives who did not support the New Democratic Party and identified as "right wing" were trying to determine which political party they could call home. Many Social Credit supporters were fiercely loyal, although most of them were also very strong and outspoken in their views against socialism. They were concerned for the economy and wanted more efficient regulation than what the NDP was instituting after their victory. Social Credit supporters wanted the NDP government back in opposition as quickly as possible. The mantra of "don't split the vote" was repeated often as a core strategy to regain government.

Coleman and Strongitharm were two people actively trying to determine which political party they should support. "For a couple of years after 1991 we all wondered what was going to happen. Social Credit had been so strong for so long, but when Grace McCarthy ran in Abbotsford, and Mike de Jong beat her running for the BC Liberals, it was obvious that the SoCreds were gone as a force," Coleman said.

Grace McCarthy was an iconic figure in the Social Credit Party from 1966 until 1991, spending all of those years as an MLA and cabinet minister, except 1972 to 1975 when the Barrett NDP government was in power and she worked in the Social Credit opposition as a staff member. She was a powerhouse with many accomplishments and her own list of controversies.[56] The fact that she lost in a part of the province that was part of the strongest base of Social Credit was a huge indicator of the party's fortunes. Mike de Jong was a newcomer to politics and beat her while running for the BC Liberals.[57] It is understandable that de Jong's victory over McCarthy in such a strong Social Credit area was a huge signal that Social Credit was not a factor in British Columbia anymore.

A key factor boosting de Jong's support was the new and well-funded leader of the BC Liberals, former Mayor of Vancouver Gordon Campbell. Campbell had taken over the leadership in a high-profile race between the incumbent leader Gordon Wilson, Gordon Gibson, who had served as a Liberal MLA in the 1970s, and two others. Campbell and his supporters had been vocal in appealing to free enterprise voters looking for a new home, and soon after taking over the leadership he changed the name to "BC Liberals" in order to indicate that in British Columbia they were different from the Liberals in the rest of the country. In addition, the logo was changed from Liberal red to red and Conservative blue, heavy on the blue, to visually demonstrate that it was a coalition of free enterprise. Even with this, there was still some strong

---

56 *Grace McCarthy, the first lady of B.C.'s Social Credit, dies at 89*, Doug Ward, *Vancouver Sun*, 2017.

57 *McCarthy edged as Campbell coasts to victory*, Times-Colonist, Victoria, B.C., February 18, 1994.

resistance to the new coalition being connected to the word "Liberal," which opened the door to another option called BC Reform. Coleman was going to have to make a choice, and make it soon, because an election was expected in 1995.

Coleman lived in Langley, near the Matsqui riding, and there was a general expectation that the riding would not vote for a party with the word "Liberal" in it. He was surprised by the by-election outcome, and still not persuaded that he was ready to move to the Liberal party. It was shortly after McCarthy's defeat and before the recalling of the legislative assembly for the spring debates that three of the remaining five Social Credit MLAs made a surprise move into a new political party called BC Reform. [58] While the BC legislature sat for debate in the spring of 1994, the BC Reform Party gained official party status when a fourth MLA left the Social Credit Party to join them.

In the Fraser Valley, where Coleman had been active since moving to Langley, there was a lot of talk about the BC Reform Party. The leader Jack Weisgerber, often referred to as "Gentleman Jack," was providing a strong and credible performance as leader of BC Reform, and with official party status Reform MLAs could speak out in Question Period and have a larger budget for research and communications. [59]

Coleman offers perspective on his choices: "At some point, Bruce and I discussed what to do. Where do we go? At that period of time, we were just involved in our jobs. The SoCreds had pretty much fallen apart. During the time when Campbell came in, I was still not a BC Liberal. I heard about a leadership debate for the Reform Party at the Aldergrove Legion. I had met Jack Weisgerber before and liked him. Bruce and I went and sat at the

---

58   *Then there was one: Serwa last Socred MLA, Times-Colonist,*Victoria, B.C., September 21, 1994.

59   *Fortune's eyes leave McCarthy glum, Gamble dazzled: [Final Edition],* Keith Baldrey, *The Vancouver Sun,*Vancouver, BC, March 15, 1994.

back of the room and looked around." He pauses. "For lack of a better description, it was a room full of old white guys."

When I was interviewing Coleman for this part of the book, I gave him a significant look when he described his concern that the room was full of, well, his own demographic. I had to point that out, and he laughed but continued, "The comments we could hear in the room from the folks behind us were just racist and nasty, the kind of thing you would read on Twitter. In the parking lot afterward, I said to Bruce, 'I don't feel like we belong there.' He agreed."

Many Social Credit operatives were very much like Coleman and Strongitharm, and I knew this because I had met so many of them in Kelowna over the years. My father Alan Tyabji's involvement with the Social Credit Party meant that my sister Josie Tyabji and I had attended community events and fundraisers with him a few times. The party thrived on the grassroots work of its members, most of whom were in the same clubs and socialized with each other. It was not a typical political party: it operated as a large family, with an amazing organizational and communication network. This is one reason why, once a decision was made for SoCred members to move into a new party, the old party almost disappeared.

Coleman, a federal Conservative, made his decision to join the BC Liberals in 1995. "There was an event at a friend of mine's house, John Scholtens,[60] and he was hosting Gordon Campbell, either before or after the Chamber meeting where Campbell was speaking. We knew a lot of the people in the room, and we thought maybe this could be a new political home." Coleman recalled that it was a good gathering with not too many people,

---

60 John Scholtens was Mayor of Langley from 1993 to 1999. Gordon
    Campbell and his team organized many of the party's candidates and
    ridings by leveraging the municipal government contacts. Campbell served
    as President of the UBCM.

and that Campbell spoke well and was very personable. The first step was taken on Coleman's path to his election as MLA for Langley, even though at the time his only ambition was to help out in the new free enterprise party.

Sheila Orr had been involved in politics for many years and met Coleman around the time that he joined the BC Liberals. "I met Rich at the very beginning of my active political life in 1994 and 1995, when I ran for the first time for the BC Liberals under Gordon Campbell. I met him there and of course we all became a family. I am known as a hardcore Liberal federally and provincially...

"From there on, I ran for the provincial Liberals three times— twice I lost, once I won. He was always there through all my campaigns. As a woman running it's tougher, especially financially. I was raising money in a riding that had been NDP for about 90 years and it was really hard, probably one of the toughest ridings in BC. Rich always supported me. I raised quite a bit of money considering, but he always made sure I had enough."

Coleman became known as one of the most successful and generous fundraisers in the history of the BC Liberals from before, during, and after his time in office.

Chapter 8
FAMILY TIES

The creation of a more peaceful and happier society has to begin from the level of the individual, and from there it can expand to one's family, to one's neighborhood, to one's community and so on.

—The Dalai Lama[61]

The foundation for Coleman's call to serve is from his parents, grandfather, and other family members. Rich's home was in Penticton from the time he was three years old until he left to join the RCMP at the age of 19. Penticton was in the southern part of the Okanagan Valley, an hour or so south of Kelowna.

He was the third of six children, five boys and one girl. His Catholic parents welcomed their sons William, Stanley, Richard, and Patrick from 1950 until 1956, and added their daughter Rosanne in 1960 and their youngest son Edward in 1961. His siblings grew up to take on careers as diverse as university professor in political science, forester, wastewater engineer, special education expert in autism policy, and CEO of Barkerville, which somehow segued into Councillor of Quesnel.

Coleman's first hero was his grandfather William Francis Stewart, his mother's father, who lived with the family in

---

61   *The Art of Happiness in a Troubled World*, Howard Cutler and the Dalai
      Lama, Penguin Random House, 2009. p.273.

Penticton. His grandfather had been a farmer until the 1930s Depression, when he lost everything and moved to the Kootenays to be a carpenter, building core boxes for the mines, later moving to Penticton and working in the boiler room of the Incola Hotel, a former CN Hotel.

"I had some work there too, later. He worked there until he was in his 70s and one day they came to him and said, 'Mr. Stewart, we had no idea how old you are, you can't really work here anymore.' And they forced him to retire, so he set up shop in the basement and built core boxes for the Kootenay mines. We boys would help him, and he would ship them out by Greyhound bus."

They had a three-bedroom house with a rumpus room downstairs. Coleman's parents had one bedroom, his grandfather had a bedroom, his sister had a bedroom, and all four boys were in bunkbeds in the converted rumpus room. Coleman didn't have his own room until he moved out.

Coleman's dad, Donald William Coleman, was a self-taught forensic accountant investigator with Revenue Canada who had sworn an oath of secrecy that, decades later, Rich would swear to become a member of the Royal Canadian Mounted Police. "He was an absolutely brilliant accountant and investigator. I got to know his work and watched him give evidence in a case once. He pulled a cheque out of a big book of briefs, and without a note he was able to say where it came from, and describe all the details, leading to a finding of income tax fraud."

His mother Rosa Coleman (née Stewart) was an English teacher who instilled a very strong sense of duty and learning in her children. The family story was that she was delivered by an Indigenous midwife on a Blackfoot reserve in Alberta.

Coleman actually attended kindergarten twice. "My mother decided she would teach us kindergarten, so from the time I was four, my older brother would leave through the back door, walk around, ring the front doorbell, and say, 'Good morning, Mrs. Coleman.' So I kicked up a fuss and was able to join in and did that for two years. In Grade 1, I had it pretty good because I had some basic skills."

Coleman's earliest memory is from when he was three years old and the family had just moved to Penticton. He was in the backyard watching his father and grandfather doing a task that to a little boy must have seemed like moving mountains. The yard had big rocks in it, and what he watched is not likely to be a scene most children would watch today.

"I sat to the side playing and watched my dad and granddad break rocks, and they built a rock wall with plants in it on the end of the yard between us and the neighbours. In child's terms it felt like a long time, but knowing them, it probably only took them a week."

The brothers were pretty competitive, and Coleman describes the neighbourhood as one that was full of young children, 28 children just on their side of the block. Still, his admiration for his grandfather often kept him around the house, where he was inspired by his work ethic. His grandfather was happiest when he was working constantly on specific and useful outcomes. There were no complaints and no need for praise.

"He was a really interesting guy. He was quiet. I just adored him. I followed him everywhere. When he was 82 or 83 he built a carport for our neighbours. One day he was standing on a picnic table trying to put up a sheet of plywood by himself when he slipped and fractured his hip. When he came home, he said, 'Boys, help me into the shop.' Then he started pointing to stuff and we grabbed it for him and next thing you know, in just a few hours, he had built himself a walker. It had a bit of a platform for the lumber so he could make his way around the shop with his supplies. Decades later, I still have some of those supplies. I took the tap and dye, the old Stanley planer."

Coleman's school years were a blend of Catholic private school and public high school. The Penticton Indian Reserve, as it was called then, was near the airport in town, and there were many Indigenous children at his school. "Two or three of my best friends in school were First Nations, most of them were bused in from three or four miles away. We would hang out, ride our bikes back to the reserve, play baseball. We were all the same. We were just kids. I would stay at their house, have dinner at their house. We hung out on weekends."

In high school, Coleman was a mediocre student, even though his parents constantly encouraged him to be more academic. He played all sports well enough, with hockey as his favourite. He managed to get into the Sea Cadets at a young age, taught Phys Ed as a summer job for two years, and joined the Glee Club, singing in musicals from grade 8 to grade 12.

There were very few indications in the demeanor of the BC Liberals' Enforcer that would suggest five years of Glee Club.

"I was an altar boy from Grade 1 or so. I never won Altar Boy of the Month. There actually was such a thing in Penticton. Both of my older brothers got Altar Boy of the Month. I never made it. I think one of them won it twice. My oldest brother won every single academic award for every single thing he was in, always. The other one was such a good athlete and a decent student. So that's what I had to follow.

"When I arrived in junior high school they thought they were getting a super student and athlete, but they got me. My parents used to say, 'You have a higher IQ than your brothers,' and then there was a point when my mom said, 'At some point in your schooling you majored in girls.'"

Coleman was born December 16, 1953, which had him graduating in 1970 at the age of 17. During his time in the Sea Cadets and the Naval Reserve he worked his way to second in command. His father had been in the military, and Coleman was attracted to a disciplined environment.

"I was in Sea Cadets for years, took a course every summer. Went to college for one semester in the fall, took general studies. I wasn't ready. So I became a roofer, which helped me later because I did roofing on weekends when I was a cop." Coleman applied the lessons he had learned at home from his grandfather.

Coleman met his wife, Michele, in Penticton at a party in the fall of 1971—the same year he graduated high school. He was interested in her right away; they started dating not long after. He began to think of long-term plans and the future. "I knew I needed to find a career. I applied for the Canadian Armed Forces and the RCMP. I applied at 18 and whichever came first was going to be my career. The Mounties to me were Canada. I'm going to go serve my country. It sounds corny but I was kind of like that."

Just 23 days after Coleman turned 19, he was in training for the RCMP. [62] "I was driven to Chilliwack by my dad, was sworn in and then put on a train to Regina. Although I was born in Nelson and had grown up in Penticton, when I got off the train in Regina, it was 30 degrees below and a blizzard. That weather I had never seen! I knew snow, but nothing like that. It was blowing snow, you can't see where you are going, and it was unbelievably cold." He graduated from the RCMP in 1973 and was the valedictorian for his troop, and his father went up and asked for a copy of his speech after he gave it. He still has a copy in his desk.

Coleman and Michele were married almost two years after he joined the RCMP. "We were engaged in 1973 in Penticton on the May long weekend. I went home because she sent me a 'Dear John' letter. So I went and bought a ring, went home and asked her to marry me. She said yes, and she was 19, I was 20 when we got married in Penticton. It was a regimental wedding. Red serge for me and my best man, and we had the lancers. When we came out of the church they crossed the lances. We married in the Catholic Church, St. Anne's. I was probably more sure than her."

---

62   Interview with Rich Coleman, February 14, 2021, by Zoom.

After Coleman graduated from the RCMP, he went to Canmore, Alberta for six months, and then he worked another six months in Calgary. Rich and Michele Coleman were married on August 31, 1974 and then on September 1, 1974 Coleman was transferred to Brooks, Alberta, where he really established himself as a police officer.[63]

---

63 Interview with Rich Coleman, February 6, 2021 by Zoom.

Chapter 9
THE WILD WEST

*The police are the frontline protectors of society. With
inadequate resources, they are asked to be enforcers,
counsellors, social workers, advisers and compassionate
friends to children and families in need, and a myriad of
other things. They have to make split-second decisions that
everyone gets to second-guess for days. The next time you
go to judge or criticize the police, ask yourself what you'd
do when confronted with a fatality, a threat to kill or a real
living crisis.*

—Rich Coleman, First Speech in
the BC Legislature, July 4, 1996

Rich and Michele lived in Brooks, Alberta for six years, and their
daughter Jacqueline was born there in 1977. Many of the stories
told about him during this time describe a character that easily
took on the role of the Enforcer when he was elected.

A former Crown prosecutor described Brooks in the 1970s
as being a pretty chaotic place. Darwin Greaves was appointed
Chief Crown Prosecutor in Medicine Hat in 1976, in 1992 he
was appointed Queen's Counsel, and in 1998 he was Appointed
Provincial Court Judge. He retired in 2019.

He describes Brooks in those days as a huge geographical area,
where most of the residents were gophers and antelopes. "Let

me tell you about Brooks—you may say it's nowhere and in the middle of nothing, but it was the epicentre of the development of gas in North America.

"Brooks was a major [area of] low-depth gas development and the place went nuts. It went absolutely nuts. There were enormous amounts of money, service rigs, oil industry, and everything else."

Where there is money like that in a new location without community, it can take some time for civilization to take hold. Greaves had a close view of exactly how it was.

"It was Dodge City. It was completely lawless. Before everyone condemns the oil and gas industry, it took them two or three years to get a hold of this craziness. Today it is the most regulated, responsible, well-managed industry, but the town at that time went crazy until the industry caught up.

"That's where the RCMP come in. In those days, they were stationed above a house, then the office moved into a mall—and they were bringing in manpower. They were expanding.

"At the front line, the RCMP had a very difficult time, the workers would often be in the bars after work with lots of disposable income. They were making $150,000 a year and the RCMP at that time was probably making $25K. A cop in Brooks in those days—everything was exploding under their feet—they were dealing with wild and crazy cowboys making five times as much money as the cops.

"In the final analysis, the industry and the RCMP got on top of it."[64]

One of Coleman's closest associates at the time was an RCMP officer named Stan Drielich, who passed away before the writing of this book. Coleman and Drielich together made a strong impression on Greaves, who made a point of saying that in the decades since Coleman left the RCMP and I contacted Greaves

---

64   Interview with Darwin Greaves, April 1, 2021, by phone.

for the book interview, Rich Coleman had never been in touch with him. Greaves's relaying of Coleman's work in Brooks in his six years of service there is not influenced by any kind of ongoing interaction, and Greaves wanted that on the record. "Since the time that Mr. Coleman came and went through my life, I have not had a single dealing or conversation with him. This is very important to understand that nothing of what I am going to say is personal. I have no relationship with Mr. Coleman at all. I have no reason to favour him. None. Zero.

"One thing to herald itself through this conversation: I have never forgotten him. He had royal jelly. I can't call him Rich, I called him Constable. I didn't know him by any other name. When I first saw him on TV as assistant premier, I thought, 'That's Coleman!' and it made perfect sense to me. I thought, 'Of course he is.'"

The context for Coleman's arrival in Brooks was the chaos that was not just in the community but also in the RCMP detachment, which had become a major station. Greaves observed that for about 15 years, there were serious managerial issues, including "mental health [concerns], alcoholism, and sheer incompetence." Greaves speaks to Coleman's role as an authority figure in the Wild West of Brooks, Alberta. His comments are definitely worthy of standing on their own:

> ...when Coleman—and you have to judge him in part in the partnership he had with Stan Drielich—who is dead now—these two people were very different, yet the same, and they formed a partnership.
>
> Drielich was more physical. I don't mean brutish, I mean he had a physical presence. They were both about the same size. Coleman was the cerebral one. Drielich would walk up and confront it. Coleman would consider it and think it out.

These two men—notwithstanding the detachment had expanded to maybe 30 men (I'm not a historian, I don't know)—these two men, and I'm not exaggerating, these two men became the detachment.

You had lawyers, prosecutors, firefighters, social workers, all contributing to the general administration of justice. There were only two men on the streets of Brooks who mattered and that was Drielich and Coleman.

If they weren't there it didn't get done right. If someone else did it, you couldn't count on it.

I'm not trying to insert any hyperbole but to give you an idea of these two and their role in Brooks, I would say Wyatt Earp and Doc Holliday. They were the force. Period.

What major trials did Rich Coleman have? I don't have a memory of any of them. I will tell you why. When Rich Coleman did something, none of us disputed it. Period. I can remember him being in court 35 times but I can't remember the trials.

No one questioned his testimony. No one questioned his integrity.

It went through court like Metamucil through my body.

He was just a really good cop.[65]

A close colleague of Coleman's at the time was Brian Sinclair, an RCMP officer who worked with him on a few incidents and has some vivid recollections. Sinclair retired from the RCMP

---

65   Interview with Darwin Greaves, ibid.

after 20 years of service and set up his own private investigation company in Calgary.

Sinclair agrees that the money and lack of rules created quite a challenge for officers. "There was a lot of drugs, there were guys making loads of money in their mid-twenties—as long as they had their apartment and their brand-new vehicle, everything else was for booze and drugs and rock and roll.

"It was an exciting time, it was a different time. I knew that if I needed assistance, I would have it. I only discharged my weapon once in 20 years. I was ready to fire on at least one other occasion, because it is a reflex, [a] trained response when your life is threatened. Fortunately, a family member took the weapon from the angry individual."

Sinclair remembers how Coleman was in the RCMP. "As a police officer, he was not a bully. He is very tall and tilts like a sailboat in the wind when he walks, but he has no swagger. He is thick-skinned enough and he lets a lot of the public comment roll off him. Some might consider his self-confidence as arrogance."

There was so much work to do keeping the peace in the 1970s that Sinclair added, "There was no overtime in those days. It wasn't a question of whether or not you were needed, you just stayed out until you got the job done. That was part of the cohesive unit that formed the Brooks detachment or any other detachment for that matter."

So many of the officers were so young. Coleman was 19 years old when he started, and Sinclair made a point of saying that when he became an RCMP officer at 23, he was considered one of the older officers.

"Here you are, you are 22 or 23. At that time you had to be two years single so they could post you where they wanted to by throwing your stuff into a suitcase and sending you off.

"There was a huge shift mentally and physically when you joined the force. You went from being a civilian [to undergoing] very intense training to not only being an enforcer but also being someone who had to wear many hats. If you were called to a domestic, you had to rely on your skills as an orator to separate these two people or be physically strong enough to wrestle with the husband. You were considered the 'authority' on site and you had to handle many varied situations as best you could. People trusted you to solve their problems," said Sinclair.[66]

Sinclair has an excellent way of describing just how clear the division is between "before" and "after" a member of the RCMP becomes an officer. "You go out to a place like Canmore or Brooks and suddenly you are in charge. There's an old expression, 'Six months ago I couldn't spell policeman and now I are one.'"

The sense of community among the police was strong, and they pulled together at work and outside of work, including working together to build their homes. There were packaged houses you could buy from Revelstoke Lumber, which would be shipped directly so that the walls and rafters were done.

According to Sinclair, "A number of members in Brooks at that time bought what we called Revy packages. About half a dozen of us had a lot—you got the concrete poured, and with help from a local experienced contractor, we would all invest… sweat equity. Rich at one time was a roofer and he helped a number of us shingle our houses.

"It was a time when the old adage of work hard/play hard was in place. We would have big gatherings with the fire department workers. [We] had an annual pig roast, a corn boil, [an] oyster BBQ sponsored by the local Catholic Church. We would all spend time together, wives and family included."

Coleman learned how to organize, command, respond, and work with others to bring order to chaos and pull together as a community to solve problems. This foundation would be relevant later in the years before and after his election.

---

66   Interview with Brian Sinclair, April 10, 2021, by Zoom and on audio.

There is a really good vignette that Greaves shares that also underscores a kind of fearlessness Coleman displays when he believes he is on the right side of a decision, and the imposing person that Coleman is, by nature.

Before Greaves was a judge he was a Crown prosecutor, and that is how Coleman interacted with him. Greaves remembers an incident that is quite unusual for a police officer in terms of how comfortable Coleman was.

"Remember he's a cop. So there was one case when I was the prosecutor and I had a meeting with the opposing lawyer in my office. The lawyer and I were arguing like hell and I guess we got a little loud. The door opens; not even a knock. Coleman steps in and he says, 'Keep it down.'

"And we did."

Chapter 10
RESILIENCE

> *No one escapes pain, fear, and suffering. Yet from pain can come wisdom, from fear can come courage, from suffering can come strength—if we have the virtue of resilience.*
>
> —Eric Greitens, *Resilience*

There were sometimes problems at work that were very hard to manage. Coleman recalls that the most difficult were the fatalities, especially dead babies. Even decades later, he has a very hard time talking about the reality of his work, and the multiple responsibilities that the RCMP had to take on that were so much harder to deal with in real life than they were as concepts in training. It was this resilient foundation that would later inform his job in government.

Coleman shares, "I remember the strong emotional impact of the first fatal accident. We had to attend autopsies in those days. We had to take blood and urine samples and send them to the RCMP lab. There were some really bad accidents. There was no coroner—when you were at the scene you were involved in way more things than a police officer is today. The first fatal accident impacts you all the way."

In the 1970s there was little thought to PTSD or the long-term effects on an officer of attending the scenes where children have died. Coleman said that later when his own children were born, some of the images and impacts would recur for him, and decades later, there would be echoes of this when his grandchildren were born.

"When Jacqueline was born, I was so scared, I would always check on her. When all the babies were born, even the grandchildren, I quietly checked to make sure they [were] breathing," Coleman said.

Brian Sinclair has done some reading on PTSD for officers:

> One of the things that bothers Rich is going to a fatal accident in Canmore. Who picked up the dead bodies? He was a 19-year-old kid.

> As a young member I have investigated SIDS [Sudden Infant Death Syndrome] deaths, where you must assume there may be inappropriate action on behalf of either or both parents. At the same time, you know they have just lost a child. It's a tightrope and you learn to walk on it.

> Another time, I had to notify a woman that her very healthy young son (25) had suffered a heart attack and had dropped dead. She [was] in a rural area. I went in, went through the cupboards to find the tea, and sat with her until a neighbour could come to the house.

> Then there was the time a man seriously harmed himself and there was blood everywhere when I arrived. He claimed he was beaten. Turned out he had attended his child's birth and had no idea how much pain his wife would suffer. Felt guilty.

> I mention the above incidents not for any benefit to myself, but to let you know these, or similar and much worse

incidents, were everyday occurrences to the members of
the RCMP.

Rich was no different as this was a situation he had to deal
with on a daily basis.[67]

Incidents like these were pretty impactful on a 19-year-old
man, and decades later, Coleman has a hard time separating which
memories belong to which of the four incidents with babies. He
knows that as a new recruit he was called out of bed all the time
between 2 am and when the new shift started at 8 am.

Coleman clearly recalls the evening when he was called to a
bowling alley. The parents had been bowling and the baby was in a
bassinet. The ruling was that the baby had SIDS and died, with no
clear explanation of why.

"You never know why; they are just gone. It is an incredible
trauma for the family. Crib death stuff, the children, going to
the autopsy of a child—you will never get this out of your head.
When you have to deal with the notification to the next of kin,
you have to manage their response, and that's your job. You don't
always realize at the time how it impacts you."

In Coleman's seven-and-a-half years as an RCMP officer
he had to attend at four autopsies on dead babies. "The biggest
impact is you had to pick the kid up when you were called to a
crib death. We took photos—the senior member did—and when
the ambulance arrive[d], you [had to] help bundle it up. How the
baby moved from the scene is blurry to me. I was in shock."

Decades later, when Coleman served as solicitor general,
his experiences as an RCMP officer prepared him for some of
the horrific incidents he would oversee, including the Robert
Pickton investigation, which turned out to be an awful mess of
serial killing on a pig farm.

---

67 Interview with Brian Sinclair, ibid.

Chapter 11
GOING HOME

There is no greater thing you can do with your life and your work than follow your passions—in a way that serves the world and you.

—Richard Branson[68]

After seven and a half years in the RCMP, six in Brooks, the Colemans left their life in Alberta to move home to British Columbia. "When I joined the RCMP, I thought it would be a lifetime career. If they had sent me back to BC, I would have stayed."

Alberta had provided a good life in many ways. Rich and Michele had built their first home and made many friends. However, after a trip to Disneyland, Rich remembers his wife saying, "I think I've had enough." He replied that if they were heading home to Penticton, he wanted to go into business. In a bit of serendipity, a small business in Penticton was put up for sale right after they moved back. Called Okanagan Security Services, it was an excellent fit.

Coleman soon discovered he was able to do well in business, immersed in the planning, strategy, and execution. "After I bought the business, I amalgamated it with a company named Invicta. We

---

68   *11 Quotes from Sir Richard Branson on Business, Leadership, and Passion*, Erika Anderson, *Forbes*, May 16, 2013

had 300 employees and survived the double-digit interest rate. We grew across three provinces, and I was on the road three weeks a month. Our head office was in Vancouver. Made sense to move to the coast as one of the weeks was in Vancouver. We had good people to run Penticton."

He sold the company to his partners in 1988. Rich started his own development business, an ambitious venture considering no one in his family had been in this business.

The Colemans decided to move to Aldergrove in 1984. Rich credits his time with Kinsmen, which he joined in 1974 in Brooks, for providing many of the skills and the network he needed to be successful in business and learn about building community. He created a new circle of friends and was soon president of the Aldergrove Kinsmen Club. As president, he learned budgeting, organization, and many skills he would not have learned if he had remained a policeman.

"The foundations of business, and the service aspect, helped me grow as a person," he said of his volunteer work with Kinsmen. It was also where he met his best friend Bruce Strongitharm, and their friendship is still part of many aspects of Coleman's personal and professional life decades later. Bruce's wife Sheryl and Rich's wife Michele became friends, and Sheryl worked for Coleman for 28 years.

"When I started the consulting firm after selling the security company, I needed someone in my office, so I hired Sheryl. At first I wouldn't hire her—didn't want to wreck a friendship by hiring a friend. She pestered me. Ginally my wife said, 'You need someone you can trust. You are both learning. You can hire loyalty and teach the rest.' She worked for me for [28] years."

It was not enough for Rich to join the club, make friends, run a business, and become club president. He also worked to rebuild the club membership by direct recruitment and community engagement. "We were knocking on doors to get food for the food bank and if a man under 40 answered the door, we would talk to him about Kinsmen and invite him to a meeting. That's how we rebuilt the club. We did quite well—we picked up 10 to 15 members each time and we got a lot of food."

Once someone agreed to attend a meeting, the members made a point of picking him up from his house to make sure he actually showed up. The club grew and so did the support for the food bank. Even after this, Coleman wanted to do more, and his journey into politics was almost inevitable once he began his first major Kinsmen project.

"I stood up at a Kinsman meeting and asked why there was no community centre in Aldergrove. I asked because my daughter's Brownies had been in a church basement," Coleman recalls.

Strongitharm remembers that time well. "Rich was already a leader at that time. Rich asked the question, 'Why don't we have a community centre?' Everyone said people had tried but not succeeded, so he said, 'Why don't I do it?' From that point, he took it on and we all joined in. We decided to do fundraisers, build it from scratch. The first fundraiser was a real success. This is what got Rich involved in politics was building the community centre and meeting the people who would help."[69]

Around this time, the Social Credit government was trying to find locations for the buildings that were no longer needed after Expo 86, which had been in Vancouver. Coleman started the process to acquire a building for the community centre but found that the Expo buildings were not built that well. So instead of taking on a free building that was a liability, he and his team turned their efforts toward obtaining a provincial government grant for $150,000, which was a large grant in the 1980s. He also had a commitment from the city government that they would match anything received from the province.

---

69   Interview with Bruce Strongitharm on March 1, 2022, by Zoom.

Strongitharm adds more perspective. "When we got involved in the community centre, it meant presentations to council, school board, MLAs.

"We made a lot of contacts. The city said they would match what we received from the province. They probably didn't know we would get $150 grand, but we did, so they had to match it. When the township came to us and said they wanted to put the library there, we said absolutely yes because we knew that was going to guarantee it would be built."

Coleman wrote the grant application and then spent time in the offices of several MLAs to garner support and make sure the funding was approved. He had a close look at the process, learned the relevance of it in building necessary amenities for the community, and was motivated to become more involved.

Coleman observed the close connection between the political organization and the elected representatives. "Constituency offices weren't apolitical back then. Half the money was the government, half was paid by political supporters of the MLA," Coleman says of the Social Credit era. "I finally got half the funds committed before the 1986 election, went to our local council, and immediately got the other half. This group of volunteers built the community centre with the funds; our kids swept the floors; we did the painting. We were hands-on and built the community centre as a group. It's still there.

"This is how I went into politics." All of this set the stage for Rich Coleman as an MLA who would emerge as the Enforcer and as a hardworking, loyal, competent member of government.

Chapter 12
TOWARD THE 1996 ELECTION

*My entry into politics started in 1986 when I ran for
council, and I lost. I made myself a commitment in 1986
that I would never run for public office again ... Sometimes
things just don't work out the same as you think they
will ... later I went to a speech by the then Leader of the
Opposition ... Afterward I went to a reception and had an
opportunity to meet and talk to him. It was at that time I
actually joined the B. C. Liberal Party because I thought
I had just met the person that could lead us back to a
coalition of people on the free enterprise side, to lead us to
government in the future. Now, I only joined the party to
be a volunteer because I had run campaigns for years, but I
still had no intention of entering politics—until about six
months later. I was standing in a food lineup for a fundraiser
for the then MLA Lynn Stephens at the Twin Rinks in
Langley, and the Premier happened to be standing beside
me in the lineup. He said: "I think you should consider
running for us." He gave me a very short explanation as to
why, and I bought it. From there became a journey that I
cannot describe to anyone in any way.*

—Rich Coleman, BC Legislature, February 17, 2011

After the New Democratic Party formed government in 1991 for the first time since December of 1975,[70] there were a couple of tumultuous years under Premier Mike Harcourt's leadership, with controversies over major legislative changes and allegations of wrongdoing in charitable fundraising. This all happened in the years before BC had fixed election dates. Although it was expected that elections would be called every four years, premiers often called elections early or late to suit their own political ends. Given all the controversy, the general election timing continued to be delayed.

Harcourt resigned in November of 1995 under a cloud,[71] opening the door for a leadership race. Glen Clark was 38 years old when he won the leadership on February 22, 1996, cruising to an easy victory in that campaign.[72] Clark brought fresh energy, youthfulness, and a different approach to the political conversation. He made a point of appealing to young voters and presenting an approachable, accessible, likable personality to the public. His populist approach led to an immediate restoration of interest in the NDP from many voters.

With the NDP winning a majority government in 1991, and Social Credit collapsing, the free enterprise supporters were motivated to find a united political party that could be their new home so they could prepare to defeat the NDP in the next election. Momentum was gathering for the BC Liberals, and money was pouring in from many sources that had previously funded Social

---

70 *In the 1970s, Social Democracy Was in Retreat. British Columbia's NDP Fought for It, Anyway,* Joël Laforest, *Jacobin,* Brooklyn, NY, January 3, 2021. https://www.jacobinmag.com/2021/01/ndp-canada-british-columbia-social-democracy-dave-barrett

71 *"I have no regrets,"* Harcourt says as 23-year career in politics ends, Justine Hunter, The *Vancouver Sun,* Vancouver, BC, November 16, 1995.

72 *Glen Clark easily wins NDP leadership. NDP roars back to life with new leadership: close election looms,* Jill St. Louis, *Canadian Press NewsWire,* Toronto, ON, February 18, 1996.

Credit. BC Reform was a factor drawing in votes in northern BC, so there was growing pressure on BC Reform not to split the vote of the free enterprise supporters. Campbell and the BC Liberals were focused on winning government in the general election called for May 28, 1996.

Another political door opened for Coleman shortly after he met Campbell in Langley. "When Gary Collins[73] decided he was not going to run again in Fort Langley–Aldergrove, moving to the riding of Vancouver–Little Mountain instead, the pressure on me was to run, and the rest is history," said Coleman.

Strongitharm remembers it took a while to convince Coleman. "I said to Rich, 'You should run.' Rich looked at me, [hemmed] and hawed. So I found some more people and we all said to him, 'You have to run.' So he said, 'OK, you go out and bring me back a bunch of signatures in a couple of weeks.' So we did that, brought that to him, and he couldn't back down.

"Even though we worked on Dan Petersen's campaign, we didn't have a lot of experience. A lot of us got involved, and Mark Bakken was the campaign manager for Rich. He is Administrator of the Township of Langley now. The Reform candidate was a veterinarian. They were so grassroots they didn't know how to campaign properly."

Coleman spoke to his wife before confirming. "Michele is pretty supportive. Once she gets past the decision, she rolls up her sleeves and gets working. If I wanted to do it, she would support me."

It was a busy and productive election campaign, and Coleman has vivid memories of election night in 1996. "I'm like a cat on a hot tin roof on election day. It was hard to sit still, so I decided I would be the one picking up people and taking them for rides to the polls. I was at the office when the scrutineers started to arrive,

---

73 Gary Collins was first elected as Gary Farrell-Collins in 1991 for the BC Liberals. He changed his name to Gary Collins for subsequent elections.

and they said, 'Rich, you have to go pick up the beer.' So I leave and I get back about 8:15, just after the polls close, and a guy in the parking lot says to me, 'You're elected!' I said, 'That's impossible.' He said, 'You're the first one elected!' I said, 'That's not possible—I've only been gone 20 minutes.' But actually he was right.

"It was announced on Global when they announced ridings and declared me elected. I was watching my riding, and I won every poll but two."

Although it was an evening for celebration in Langley, Coleman said they were watching the provincial results and wondering whether they were in government or opposition. They were surprised when Glen Clark won a second term for the NDP, since the NDP had never had two terms in government in BC history.

Glen Clark summed up the NDP win with an iconic phrase and a big smile. "Was that close or what?!" The BC Liberals had won more of the popular vote, but because of how the votes were distributed in the ridings, the NDP had captured a majority government.[74]

The BC Liberals had expected to be in government. They were re-elected as the official opposition with 33 MLAs, and the New Democratic Party, led by Glen Clark, won a second majority government with 39 MLAs. Two other political parties elected MLAs: the BC Reform Party elected Jack Weisgerber in Peach River South and Richard Neufeld in Peace River North, and the PDA elected Gordon Wilson in Powell River–Sunshine Coast. The BC Liberals won 2.37% more of the popular vote than the NDP's 39.45%, with 41.82%, and many of them were very loud and angry about this for a long time after the election.[75]

---

74 *Glen Clark's '96 Win, and Lessons for Today, Yes, Gordon Campbell choked. Here's how the NDP helped him do it,* Bill Tieleman, *The Tyee,* Vancouver, BC, May 31, 2016. https://thetyee.ca/Opinion/2016/05/31/Glen-Clark-96-Lessons/

75 *NDP wins majority in B.C. election: [Daily: Vancouver Edition],* Keith Damsell, *Financial Post,* Toronto, Ont, May 29, 1996.

Coleman observed, "I don't think it's as hard on people who have been elected for the first time. I don't think it was as hard on me as on those who were running for the second time, expecting they were going to be in government. Everyone thought the BC Liberals should win it, but we didn't, so [then] we had to shift gears."

A new era in BC politics had begun. Although the Social Credit Party ran candidates in 38 of the 75 ridings in 1996, which was the same number of candidates as the Natural Law Party, they received only 0.40% of the vote in the election. For a party that had held government for so long, it was a stunning collapse. For comparison, two parties that were in a general election for the first time outperformed Social Credit. The BC Reform Party of British Columbia ran 75 candidates and received 9.27% of the votes cast, and Gordon Wilson's new political party the Progressive Democratic Alliance (PDA) ran 66 candidates and received 5.74%.

Rich Coleman's 24-year career as a Member of the Legislative Assembly of British Columbia had begun. "I ran in 1996 for the first time provincially for the BC Liberals and won."

Chapter 13
OPPOSITION

*"This anonymous clan of slack-jawed troglodytes has cost
me the election, and yet if I were to have them killed, I
would be the one to go to jail. That's democracy for you."*

—Mr. Burns, *The Simpsons*

The BC Liberals had expected to win the election, and although
they picked up many more MLAs and expanded their caucus, they
were once again in opposition to the NDP. After losing the general
election, speculation was rampant that BC Liberal leader Gordon
Campbell would resign as leader, and that the new Liberal caucus
would erupt with in-fighting and dissent after the disappointing
election outcome. However, all reports of events following the
election were that the caucus and party were united and focused
on being an effective official opposition.

As B.C. Liberal leader Gordon Campbell entered his party's
first caucus meeting Friday he was greeted with the signs
of solidarity: Thirty-two standing, applauding and cheering
MLAs anxious to get started in their new jobs.

Many were like rookie MLA Geoff Plant, who, when
asked if the Liberals continue to back Campbell after
Tuesday's electoral defeat, replied: "Entirely, completely and

without reservation."

After the inspiring welcome, Campbell returned the gesture.

"I think we've got a great group of people here that are going to do a hell of a job for British Columbians."

The outward show of unity after this week's narrow election defeat appears to be more than just a public performance ... Friday's caucus meeting was more like basic training for the MLAs—20 of the 33 Liberals are new to provincial politics...[76]

Not long after this, Campbell set up a shadow cabinet, with all 32 of the Liberal MLAs receiving portfolios. Prominent MLAs were listed in news stories, and Coleman did not rate a mention in any regional coverage of the new Official Opposition.

The 33-member official Opposition, more than double its pre-election size, will also have more clout in terms of staff and research budgets...The party's budget for support staff and research, which is directly proportionate to the number of its MLAs, will jump to roughly $2.2 million annually from $1.3 million.[77]

Three MLAs also took on positions as officers: Campbell appointed Gary Collins as the house leader and Wilf Hurd as

76 *Liberal caucus gives Campbell standing ovation: The show of unity following the narrow election defeat looks like the real thing as there is little evidence of discontent,* Jim Beatty, *Vancouver Sun,* Vancouver, BC, June 1, 1996.

77 *All 32 Liberal MLAs join 'shadow cabinet': The party's budget for support staff and research will increase to $2.2 million annually, The Vancouver Sun,* Vancouver, BC, June 21, 1996.

whip.[78] The third officer position was elected by the caucus, and this is the position of caucus chair. It is an important position because of the high level of administrative responsibility and the need for the chair to be skilled in human resources and people management. The caucus elected Rich Coleman.

"I became caucus chair shortly after the election in 1996. It was an elected position. There were a couple of ballots, and then I was caucus chair. We had our first caucus meeting shortly after. I went into the office beside the large meeting room [and] used my experience in Kinsmen to write up the first agenda, which included the leader's update; house leader's update on the legislative agenda; whip's report in terms of scheduling, new business, or bills; items for discussion. I was just making it up."

Coleman had excellent support. "I wrote it up and gave it to a young man Hoong Neoh, who had set up the BC Liberal computer system and data management system. He was a legislative assistant at the time and worked for four MLAs, including me. We used blue paper for it, and this became the template for our meetings. It is still used to this day."

Bruce Strongitharm remembers this process well. "In the early days when Rich was first elected, he had no idea what his role would be in opposition. He was nervously anxious, as anyone would be. He was the housing critic, then he took on forestry. Becoming caucus chair really boosted his confidence because the position is elected by the caucus."

Coleman's time in business, political campaigning, and community organization had created a good foundation. "The reality was he was really good at running meetings. He knew how to run the meeting properly and he had confidence in the outcome."

There were no set procedures when the BC Liberals began. Even though there were a number of conventional ideas and

---

78   *Critics' roles go to Chong, Coell*, Les Leyne, *Times-Colonist*, Victoria, BC, June 21, 1996.

parliamentary procedures, how to run a meeting was at the discretion of the caucus chair. Coleman had not expected to be a key player, and certainly the media had not written him up as anyone of any significance. Strongitharm says, "He had no idea of being in the inner circle. If they had been government, he didn't expect to be in cabinet, but he knew how to get things done."

After a one-year term as caucus chair, Coleman was appointed the caucus whip, a key position of authority in managing the other MLAs, and served in that position for four years.

During Glen Clark's term, there were many huge political developments. Gordon Wilson, former leader of the Liberal Party of BC, crossed the floor of the legislature to join the NDP at the end of Glen Clark's tenure as leader of the NDP in 1999. Wilson had been defeated by Campbell as Liberal Leader in 1993, and there was a clear and deep antagonism between them. Wilson's move heightened the division between the BC Liberals and the NDP.

Wilson joined the NDP as Minister Responsible for BC Ferries and Minister of Aboriginal Affairs. At that time, these were two of the most controversial portfolios. As leader of the PDA, Wilson had caused a lot of the fuss over ferries by being the most vocal critic of Clark's "fast cats," and Gordon Campbell's BC Liberals had caused the biggest fuss in Aboriginal Affairs over the proposed Nisga'a Treaty. Campbell and some of his key critics had launched a lawsuit trying to block the passage of the Nisga'a Treaty, and it was up to Wilson to get it passed in the legislature before the coming election.

Wilson remembers Coleman clearly. "He was a part of the Campbell organization, somebody who carried a fair amount of political clout in the caucus. Coleman was, if not a leader, a deputy. Even sitting in the opposition benches, it was obvious he carried a significant amount of influence.

"When sitting in government you can see the dynamic between the caucus members who are the least influential versus those in the front benches. There was a perception that one person you don't cross is Coleman. This impression was even when he was in opposition. What I noticed is that in the Estimates debates he was well informed and well prepared. In Question Period he was someone who went to the heart of the matter quickly.

"Even though Rich Coleman was not a lead voice in the Nisga'a debate, he was a voice in that debate, along with Geoff Plant, who was the lead, and Christy Clark, who was vocal. My impression at that time was that Coleman had bought the party position hook, line, and sinker and was doing his job as a loyal soldier."[79]

The years from 1996 to the 2001 election were very heavily partisan, and divisive, with strong battle-lines drawn on key issues. The BC Liberals and the BC Reform Party fought the passing of the Nisga'a Treaty with every device possible, before and after the 1996 election. For political reasons, the BC Liberals could not afford to give up any ground on the far-right side of the debate. BC had the unusual circumstance of a former Liberal leader squaring off with a current Liberal leader. In order to pass BC's first modern-day treaty, Wilson had to invoke closure on the debate. It was widely controversial, especially in the context of the political volatility at the time: Glen Clark was low in the polls and Wilson was openly called a "turncoat" from the party he had revived and led back to opposition in 1991.

The controversial Nisga'a Treaty cleared a major hurdle late yesterday when the B.C. legislature gave it final passage.

The final vote, after the NDP government imposed closure on debate, was 38-32.

The vote split strictly along party lines, although Premier Glen Clark had for months advertised it as a free vote.

---

79   Interview with Gordon Wilson, May 11, 2021, in person.

The Nisga'a Treaty is the first modern-day land-claims settlement in B.C. and is expected in many ways to serve as a template for dozens of treaties now being negotiated...

But the Liberals remained bitter that the NDP had decided to cut off debate with dozens of clauses of the treaty awaiting detailed study and debate in the house. "No questions, no answers, no debate, no democracy... it's totally auto-cratic," said Liberal leader Gordon Campbell.

So unhappy were the Liberals that they marched out of the legislature...

The Liberals had from the beginning urged a provincial referendum on the treaty, something both the New Democrats and the Nisga'a themselves refused.

Aboriginal Affairs Minister Gordon Wilson, who took over the ministry in the middle of the Nisga'a debate when he made the switch from the Progressive Democratic Alliance to the NDP, said there had been time to debate the bill thoroughly. In fact, he noted, the treaty has been debated for longer than any other single piece of legislation in B.C. history—more than 120 hours in total.

Wilson said there also has been plenty of opportunity for public consultation, through everything from a Web site to meetings in the Northwest and around the province...

"It's on to Ottawa," said a happy Nisga'a Chief Joe Gosnell yesterday. "This is a big hurdle overcome."[80]

---

80   *House passes Nisga'a treaty: Liberals walk out of legislature in protest after NDP imposes closure on marathon debate*, Ian Austin and Barbara McLintok, *The Province*, Vancouver, BC, April 23, 1999.

Regardless of the antagonism between the NDP government Wilson represented and the BC Liberals Coleman represented, Wilson developed considerable respect for Coleman's way of tackling issues. "Coleman, in Question Period, was one of the most informed, competent, and piercing of the commentators. Where others were full of sound and fury, Coleman was always quiet, reserved, to the point, and piercing in his questions because he went to the heart of the issues. It was very hard not to answer his questions because they would pop the rhetorical bubble and get to the meat of the subject.

"What I remember in the years between 2001 and 2013, as someone observing from outside the political theatre, is how omnipresent Coleman was. He was the figure who was very much the face of the government."[81]

---

81   Interview with Gordon Wilson, ibid.

Chapter 14
THE "FUDGE-IT BUDGET" CONTROVERSY

In our age there is no such thing as "keeping out of politics." All issues are political issues, and politics itself is a mass of lies, evasions, folly, hatred and schizophrenia.

—George Orwell

Manufactured scandals prohibit public servants from doing the job they were elected or appointed to do.

—Charles B. Rangel

It was not long after the Glen Clark NDP government was sworn in that a major and defining controversy hit the headlines. This one became known as the Fudge-It Budget. The election was in May, the new government and opposition were in place in June, and by July the expected surplus budget, a key campaign promise, was a growing deficit.

As a wedge issue, it was perfect. The BC Liberals could brand the NDP as irresponsible and dishonest, provided the BC Liberals could show that the NDP had the intention to mislead the public in the election. From this first controversy and on through the full 24 years of Coleman's elected life, he was the Enforcer for the Liberals, enforcing whatever the government line was at the time and speaking without apology to the scandals, policies, issues, or events. Coleman spoke with authority and did not back down from the tough questions.

The BC Liberal opposition was at work digging into any related research that could point to Glen Clark knowingly misleading the public, and in the legislature Coleman raised allegations that Finance ministry staff were involved in deliberately presenting numbers that were not accurate. The NDP refused to answer him, and any staff who could have answered had left government. Auditor General George Morfitt was conducting a full review of what had happened and how the facts were so far removed from reality.

The BC Press Gallery's senior provincial affairs columnist Vaughn Palmer covered Coleman's questions about Premier Glen Clark's senior advisor Tom Gunton and the lunch he had with senior Finance ministry staff during the preparation of the controversial budget.

...The lunch was disclosed to the house by Rich Coleman, Liberal MLA for Fort Langley-Aldergrove. He brandished an expense statement showing that on March 12, 1996, Mr. Gunton had lunch at the cabinet offices in Vancouver with finance officials Brenda Eaton, Lois McNabb and Tom Workman. The topic was "business lunch, re budgets."

...Ms. Eaton, who held the title of acting deputy minister and head of treasury board, was the senior official in finance. Ms. McNabb, the head of fiscal and economic analysis, was in charge of forecasts of revenues and expenditures. Mr. Workman was director of communications, in charge of presenting the budget story to the news media and the public.

Mr. Gunton had no official position within the finance ministry. His title at the time was deputy minister of the environment... he'd been serving as Mr. Clark's chief adviser and emissary, and none of the other three would have had any doubt that when Mr. Gunton spoke he did so with the full authority of the premier of B.C....

...Ms. McNabb's office of fiscal and economic analysis had delivered a three-page memo advising that the economy had gone into the "tank" in the fourth quarter of the 1995. It... went on to explain how, as a consequence, the economy was unlikely to deliver anticipated revenues in either year.

In reply, Ms. Eaton made no attempt to dispute the doom and gloom projections from her staff. "We've repeatedly made that point."

...it is a matter record that, later in the day, Mr. Gunton's boss, Premier Clark, met with reporters to deliver an entirely different message... "We're on track for a balanced budget for the 1995 fiscal year and a second balanced budget next year."

Neither budget was on track. Neither ended up balanced. And if the finance ministry officials were candid in their budget lunch with Mr. Gunton, then the premier's office was already apprised of the situation...[82]

There were controversies on both sides of the legislature. In the first two years of Coleman's first term as MLA, his name was

---

82 *Lunch with Tom Gunton: Who said what about the budget?*, Vaughn Palmer, *The Vancouver Sun*, Vancouver, BC, April 29, 1997.

in the headlines connected to controversy, rather than his work. While the BC Liberals alleged financial wrongdoing by the NDP, the NDP threw allegations right back at the BC Liberals.[83] The NDP claimed that the BC Liberals had misused taxpayer money from their official opposition budget by sending out a letter and survey to 750,000 households that had a political agenda embedded in it, including claims of "mismanagement, incompetence, and dishonestly" by the NDP government.

Campbell responded to the NDP's attacks by submitting the claims to the auditor general for a full review of this activity, and Coleman was the messenger who had to answer to the public when Morfitt found that the Liberals had in fact broken the rules. Coleman then spoke on behalf of the Liberals to say that regardless of the findings, they were not paying the money back.

> The Liberal Party broke legislature guidelines for mailing privileges when it sent a partisan letter and survey to 750,000 households at taxpayers' expense, the auditor general says...

> Costing more than $700,000, it included a letter from Campbell plus a survey and a petition form asking voters to "send Glen Clark a message—we've had enough."

> ...Campbell was golfing at a charity tournament in Vancouver on Thursday and was unavailable for comment.

> Liberal caucus chairman Rich Coleman accepted Morfitt's report and challenged the NDP to submit its mailouts to Morfitt's scrutiny.

---

83   *Liberals violated guidelines, refuse to pay back the money [Auditor General]*, Wendy Cox, *Canadian Press NewsWire*, Toronto, ON, July 10, 1997.

Coleman said the Liberals do not plan to cough up for the January mailings. The party had simply followed the same past practice as the NDP, which has sent out similar partisan letters, he said.[84]

Coleman came out publicly to challenge the NDP to open up their mailings to a review, claiming that the same findings would apply, that they had misused tax dollars on partisan mailouts. The NDP agreed to adopt the findings for future mailouts but did not put their mailings up for review.

Being in the spotlight to take the heat started early for Coleman and continued throughout his career. Global BC's Legislature Bureau Chief Keith Baldrey noticed Coleman's evolution. "One of the first times I interviewed him was when he was in opposition. He was nervous. He was sweating. And I thought, 'Oh, he's going to have a tough time on camera while he is elected.' Instead, he became very comfortable. He could take the bright lights and it was water off a duck's back. He grew into the role, from a media point of view."[85]

---

84   *Liberal survey broke rules, auditor general says*, Malcom Curtis, *Times-Colonist*, Victoria, BC, July 11, 1997.

85   Interview with Keith Baldrey, December 7, 2023, by Zoom.

Chapter 15
2001 ELECTION

[People have been] ... waiting a long time for a vision
for British Columbia—a vision that will change their
children's future, a vision that will change their businesses'
futures, a vision that they can look back on and say, as
the birthplace of British Columbia, that we can now look
forward to greatness in B.C. once again ... here we are today,
part of the cusp of the true vision of great government in
Canada. We will be here in four years, having taken a pen
and checked off the plan. We will be here telling British
Columbians that for the first time in the history of B.C. a
government was elected that was accountable, that followed
through and did exactly what it promised to do. We'll all be
proud of it on that day.

—Rich Coleman, BC Legislature, August 7, 2001

The years between 1996 and 2001 were intense for the Glen Clark government. In addition to the Fudge-It Budget scandal that hit the government from the first session in the legislature, there were issues in almost every sector from housing to forestry to education that the BC Liberals raised with unrelenting pressure. The core message that the BC Liberals hammered home was that the Clark government was illegitimate because it had received fewer votes; untrustworthy because the NDP stole from charities; and dishonest because it lied during the election about the budget.

Glen Clark was under attack directly as the face of the government and the leader who had turned the fortunes around. My second book, *Daggers Unsheathed: the Political Assassination of Glen Clark*, outlines the entire story including the high-profile Total Recall campaign to try to use recall to remove some of the MLAs from office.

Recall and initiative[86] are two democratic devices that were adopted after 80% of voters supported them during a referendum held on October 17, 1991 as a vote during the general election. The Liberals under Gordon Wilson had opposed the Recall and Initiative Act, citing it as disruptive of government. The NDP enacted the legislation in their first term in government, and by their second term, recall was a tool that could remove MLAs and force out an "illegitimate" government. In 1998, the person leading this campaign on behalf of the general public was Kevin Falcon, at that time unelected. He was able to generate a lot of publicity and support for it.

Regardless of the controversies, the government had to continue to govern. Glen Clark held on as long as he could, intending to lead the NDP into the next election; however, his own Attorney General Ujjal Dosanjh made a comment that Clark was under criminal investigation, and this forced Clark's resignation. Dosanjh ran for leader of the NDP and won the leadership. He then ran a disastrous campaign and the NDP was resoundingly defeated, with only Joy MacPhail and Jenny Kwan re-elected, going from government down to two MLAs.

There was a lot at stake in the 2001 election that Kinsella chaired. Coleman was involved and all the strategy was focused on the win. They had a bit more time than expected to prepare for the election. "We assumed that the NDP would be in for a

---

86 Recall and Initiative Act, RSBC 1996 https://www.bclaws.gov.bc.ca/civix/document/id/complete/statreg/96398_02

four-year term, but it became clear they were going to hang on an extra year because they were in trouble. There was an upheaval in the NDP over Glen Clark's issues. When the four years became five years, we were not happy."

Patrick Kinsella is a seasoned Conservative political strategist and corporate consultant with decades of experience in campaigns, even once being referred to as "The Ultimate Mr. Fixit" in Canada's national newspaper.[87] Leaders have relied on his advice frequently and he is careful in how he spends his time, money, and words. From the time he connected with Coleman, they began to work together, became friends, and often socialized together. Their wives also became friends.

"After the 1996 election, Gord realized he was outmanoeuvred by Glen Clark... Glen Clark got on his motorcycle and rode around the province and out-campaigned us. I wasn't involved in '96, but when I got involved in 1998, I remember Gord saying, 'I don't want that to ever happen again. I want good candidates. I want to be financially ready. I want to know all the details.' Rich took the overview that was more strategic in terms of how do we win this election and what are the issues.[88]

"I knew Rich as a federal Tory back in the '80s because I was working with the Mulroney campaign in 1984 and '88. He was a conspicuous federal Conservative. I didn't keep in touch until I discovered he was going to run in 1996. In 1998 Campbell asked if I would get involved, and I ended up chairing the campaign in 2001. We had a war room downtown where we set up office. I got to know Rich in [those] years between 1998 and 2001. Rich is a very loyal person."

Coleman was safe in his own seat, and it was generally known that he could get re-elected pretty easily, although he never took it

87   *Patrick Kinsella is the ultimate Mr. Fixit*, Robert Matas, *The Globe and Mail*, Vancouver, BC, January 5, 2012.

88   Interview with Patrick Kinsella, April 30, 2021, by Zoom.

for granted. The team who worked for him had been with him for years, even before his time in politics. Kinsella noted, "He is the ultimate team player, likes people around him, likes to be the centre of it.

"Rich was more of a strategist on the overall story of the campaign itself. He was interested in activities affecting him as a critic. He wanted to follow how the NDP government was managing and how we could have a strategy to defeat them based on their governing."

Meanwhile, Campbell was laser-focused on the biggest win possible. "Gord had the tactics figured out from the get-go, that we could win every seat. Rich was a big part of that in terms of how to roll the campaign out by riding. He was the first one to understand that the NDP had done it to themselves and we were more than ready to pounce in and take over. Rich was a big part of the strategic overview of, 'How do we win this?'"[89]

Gordon Campbell was elected premier in a historic landslide on May 16, 2001, with 77 MLAs elected out of 79 ridings, and only two political parties in the legislature. His new government had a difficult job to do: Create a cabinet with so many people competing for an important spot and a campaign promise of efficient government.

With the memorable quote "BC is back and we are ready to go," Gordon Campbell made history as the premier-elect of British Columbia in a record-breaking victory. On election night, it was announced as 76 Liberals to 3 NDP members, but after a recount, the NDP lost the seat in the capital city of Victoria. BC's pre-eminent political columnist, Vaughn Palmer of the *Vancouver Sun*, summed it up in the context of BC's previous elections.

> The leader ranked by history as the master of B.C. politics, W.A.C. Bennett, won his most impressive victory in 1969, scooping 47 per cent of the popular vote and finishing 21 seats ahead of the combined opposition parties.

---

89   Interview with Patrick Kinsella, ibid.

His son Bill, who built a broader coalition, came close to capturing 50 per cent of the popular vote in three successive elections. In his most personally satisfying win in 1983, he finished with 13 seats more than the New Democratic Party.

When Bill Vander Zalm breezed to an easy win over lacklustre NDP leader Bob Skelly in 1986, some called it a landslide. By the numbers, he finished with 25 more seats and a seven-point edge in the popular vote.

And the word "decisive" was often applied to the outcome in 1991, when Mike Harcourt's New Democrats captured 27 seats more than the combined opposition—though the NDP did it with just 40 per cent of the popular vote.

But we'll have to come up with a new set of words to describe the result of election 2001. You want "impressive," "satisfying," "decisive" and "landslide?"

As I typed these words shortly after 9 p.m. last evening, the Liberals were elected and leading in 76 of the 79 seats in the provincial legislature.

He and the Liberals wiped out the NDP government—ministers, backbenchers, newcomers and veterans alike. The premier was beaten. Ditto the two men he defeated for the party leadership, Corky Evans and Gordon Wilson.[90]

Campbell's speech on election night set the tone for his time in office and provided Coleman and the rest of the caucus with a clear mandate.

90   *B.C. is back and we are ready to go,* Vaughn Palmer, *The Vancouver Sun,* Vancouver, BC, May 17, 2001.

After eight years as premier-in-waiting, Gordon Campbell finally delivered the victory his supporters had been expecting Wednesday.

"Welcome to a new era for all British Columbia," he croaked in a hoarse voice.

"B.C. is back and we are ready to go," he told more than 1,000 cheering supporters who crowded into the ballroom of the Wall Centre Hotel in downtown Vancouver.

With his voice almost gone, he promised again to keep the commitments he made during the campaign.

"I want everyone to know, that we will not let you down," he said.

"We are committed to building a thriving economy, a superb health care system that is second to none so British Columbia is leading again."

Campbell called his victory a "triumph of optimism and hope," and pledged to work to create the open government he promised during the campaign, despite his massive victory.

"We are going to reform our institutions, we're going to make them work for you and I'm going to count on you to help me do that and take this message across this great province."[91]

---

91   *'We will not let you down': The premier-elect vows to keep campaign promises*, Craig McInnes, *The Vancouver Sun*, Vancouver, BC, May 17, 2001.

Chapter 16
GOVERNMENT

Democracy, to me, is not about browbeating people with your opinions. It is not about demeaning others because they have an opinion that differs a wee bit from yours. It is not about making decisions in any other manner than through courtesy, listening, fairness and legitimate debate. I believe that we must do this as elected officials in this province... People measure us by what they see; they measure us by whether they think we are a reflection of their values. We need to recognize a diversity of opinion and positions that, frankly, leads us to solutions through some confrontation, with the allowance to be able to do it and do it fairly... I think those values of honesty, integrity, and the ability to listen and debate and discuss with some integrity are something that should never be lost on us, should never be lost on this House and should never be lost in our communities.

—Rich Coleman, December 2, 1998, BC Legislature

From the beginning, Rich Coleman was in the inner circle, with a cabinet position. Coleman was appointed minister of public safety and solicitor general on June 5, 2021, in the first cabinet of Premier Gordon Campbell. BC had not had a solicitor general since 1971, when the NDP appointed Alex Macdonald. The news stories reported that Coleman was a loyal soldier who would not amount to anything.

Strongitharm remembers the appointment well. "It seemed they thought he was a guy with very little education, a guy who was a cop, how could he be solicitor general? Because he was big, some people were intimidated, and in the legislature sometimes he would get excited so people would think he was hard to work with, but actually he had no staff turnover at all. As solicitor general, he handled himself really well. When he got material from the ministry staff, he always read it, comprehended it, and asked for ideas from the staff and followed up. Staff liked being around him."[92]

Three months and six days after Coleman became solicitor general, the world changed when the twin towers in New York fell to a terrorist attack. Coleman was in charge of BC's response. The emergency started early on the morning of September 11, 2001. The first airplane hit the north tower of the Twin Towers in New York at 8:46 a.m. Eastern time. About 15 minutes later, the second airplane hit the south tower.

"When 9/11 hit, I had a call from my deputy minister Kevin Bane. We talked about how the airplane hit one tower and they closed the airport. I saw the second plane hit the tower while we were talking. He said, 'You might want to come down to the office.'"

Coleman was the new solicitor general with an unprecedented situation. He had to work with his senior staff and all the leaders of emergency services to put systems in place, and immediately. They needed to create the full documentation for a regional state of emergency, and it had to dovetail into the larger plans for Canada, the United States, and any other jurisdiction with which he was interacting.

92   Interview with Bruce Strongitharm, March 18, 2022, in person.

"We booked every hotel available between Vancouver and Chilliwack. We had all these planes coming to Vancouver—6000 people in total on these planes—we had to process all of them and find them somewhere to stay."

That day, just over an hour after a major global catastrophe, he had to walk into cabinet at 10:00 to tell them what he planned to do. As minister, it was his responsibility to oversee a successful plan, but Coleman said the staff were key to the plan and its execution.

"9/11 happened in September. I was paged when the first plane hit, and there were 6000 people in the air heading to Vancouver. I had to declare a state of emergency and we were on the phone working on grounding the planes and sorting out the passengers when the second plane hit," Coleman explained. "We had to move fast to book all the hotels and sort out the logistics for transportation."[93]

In addition to dealing with passengers, Coleman was tasked with moving every employee out of the United States Consulate. "Not only did they say to get everyone out of the air, I had a phone call saying that the US Consulate needed a boost, their security wasn't big enough for the risk level. So we added the employees to the list of people we had to sort out."

Coleman had already been working on emergency preparedness as one of his core mandates as solicitor general. He had been questioned on the resources for this previously and had replied that you do this because when an emergency happens, the strategic thinking is in place and you can move quickly.

As for ensuring 6000 passengers and the entire US Consulate were sorted out, Coleman says, "We just got it done. By the time I reported out to cabinet that day, we had already booked every hotel between Vancouver and Chilliwack for the grounded passengers and deployed the plan for the Consulate."

---

93   Interview with Rich Coleman, February 2, 2021, by Zoom.

The scale of the emergency and the efficiency of the response set the stage for Coleman's role in the BC Liberal government over the next 16 years. "I wasn't always putting out fires. I was often just getting things done. I would get this call—we have this issue, can you help? The answer was always yes.

"It was my job."

Vaughn Palmer knew Coleman quite well during his entire time in office. "We don't pay enough attention to British Columbia politics to really remember anyone who isn't premier. Occasionally we remember a figure like Bob Williams, Grace McCarthy, or Moe Sihota. Under Campbell I guess you would have to say Coleman because he stayed the whole time. He was the most powerful minister through the Campbell government although he was never finance minister."[94]

Palmer hosted a political news program called *Voice of BC*. "For 20 years I had a TV show, with an hour to interview politicians. Coleman was a regular guest. You could ask him anything and he stood fast, told you what he thought, why he did it that way. He was straightforward.

"He never strayed away from the issues or the controversies. At the cabinet table for 16 years, Coleman was always one of the strongest defenders of the government and what it was doing. He was not known for dodging the question."[95]

In cabinet and as MLA, Coleman focused on absorbing as much information as he could on as many issues as were in front of him. He developed a reputation for being prepared. "When I first became a minister, I would read the binder the night I received it. It took the bureaucrats a while to realize that when they came in to brief me, I had already read the material, wasn't going to have them read it to me or go through it. That's how you get things done. You have to be prepared."

94   Interview with Vaughn Palmer, December 6, 2023, by Zoom.
95   Palmer, ibid.

Coleman had been successful in business. To serve as a cabinet minister, he had to put his business assets in trust or divest them. There was a price for this. "Financially, it was the worst decision to become a cabinet minister," he told me. "But it was also the best decision I ever made, crap or not, to be able to get so much done. It's the things you can do for people locally."

There was also a strategy to success in the halls of power. Palmer recalls that power was tightly held in the Campbell government. "The three most powerful people in BC were Campbell, followed by Martyn Brown, followed by Lara Dauphiney, who did scheduling. Would Coleman think he was the most powerful minister? Probably not, but he probably was."

While Coleman is extremely humble and tends to understate his power, he was definitely aware that his strategies were effective at delivering results. He spoke in the legislature a lot and he did not need help doing his speeches. He would identify and solve problems.

"One thing you learn as a minister: If it is policy, you can change it quickly; If it is regulation, it is six months; If it is legislation, it is two years. So you look for ways to make quick changes. Also, I would try not to have the leader in the middle of a scandal or controversy."

Keith Baldrey thinks Rich is a very personable, likable character. "He was very dependable. I have a story that shows what Coleman was like in fixing problems.

"There was an issue with single, disabled women on assistance who were having benefits clawed back if they had spousal support payments. It became an issue in the ledge. NDP's Michelle Mungall brought it out.

"Coleman sought me out in the hallway and said, 'OK, what is this?'

"Question Period is a lot of noise, not a lot of substance, so he wanted more info, and from a non-partisan source. I told him these women are basically getting screwed through no fault of their own.

So he said, 'OK, we're going to fix this.' And in the next budget, it was fixed. It didn't get a lot of publicity but it was an example of Coleman, behind the scenes, finding a mess and cleaning it up."[96]

96   Interview with Keith Baldrey, December 7, 2023, by Zoom.

Chapter 17
PUBLIC SAFETY

Policing operations are going to have to be cost-effective.
They're going to have to be accountable to you and
accountable to society. There have to be ethical standards
for police members across the board … The public have the
right to believe that we have transparency in policing—
transparency in the way we will deal with police forces
and their members—and that we will provide them in the
future with the professional development, the organization
and the priorities that make sense to deal with the crime in
this country, and not the wrong agendas. That will be very
critical to policing, and I hope the organizations such as
the RCMP and municipal forces are prepared to make the
adjustments and changes so that they will be able to do this
in the future.

—Rich Coleman, BC Legislature, April 5, 2000

When Coleman was appointed to the position of solicitor general on June 5, 2001, he was generally described as a loyal soldier who will never amount to anything. Part of his responsibility list was public safety. He tackled this with the insights he had gained from private life, starting with transition houses.

"Transition houses didn't have funding for 24-hour staff. This needed to be fixed, so we added funding for that. Gave them more stability. Tough to ask volunteers to be there at midnight, especially when that is when a lot of domestic violence occurred. We added more facilities and more services."

It was not his work as a police officer that gave him the perspective of what was needed to make transition houses better; it was his time running his security business. "It struck me that the facilities had to be staffed when people were at greatest risk. Families could only go for short stays—I learned that in my business. I knew we needed second-stage housing. So that after the 30 days they had somewhere safe to go."

Coleman had started projects for second-stage housing during his years with Kinsmen in the 1980s, and although other non-profits picked up on it, there was always a waiting list for social housing.

Also in his portfolio were police and correctional services. Coleman visited every site at different locations around BC and decided which would stay and which would go. He did consolidations and moved resources around based on his direct observations.

Coleman transformed policing in BC. He tells the story of that process in his own words:

> When I became the minister, I was handed policing. The state of policing in 2001 was abysmal. When I took over we were about 150 officers short in BC. They were managing the underfunding by vacancy. We had places where if someone was away on holidays, you only had one person for hundreds of miles. I helped fix all of that. I put money into anti-homicide, integrated organized crime, and other important areas.
>
> First, I met with the Deputy Commissioner of RCMP for BC. There are only a few in Canada. BC was big enough to have one. Bev Busson was the first female Commissioner for

the RCMP of Canada. After she retired, she was appointed to the Senate … Our first meeting was a bit tense. I told her what she needed to do was hire an accountant to give me a financial report of what I needed to do, and I would take it to cabinet for funding.

We worked through the budget. I got the numbers [and] took [them] to government, and we reinvigorated the police force in BC. They were running their cars 50 to 60K longer than they should have. With the budget increase, there was now funding for basic equipment that they had not had for a long time; they had no certainty previously, because the previous government would fund in the budget but claw the funds back before they were spent.

So then I said to her, now that you have your needs met, what else? We kept working together.

We needed 911 to be more efficient, so I amalgamated the systems. I had had the experience when I was RCMP in Alberta where we couldn't talk to each other if we were in different jurisdictions. So if we were in a high-speed chase and we needed to talk to the Calgary police, we had to talk to our radio room who would have to relay it to the police by phone.

In BC the police still had firewalls between jurisdictions. I'm sitting with the missing women's file—we hadn't found Pickton at this point—but the system in the '90s was one where it was reported to Vancouver and they would send a fax out to other police departments. Jim Chu, who would later become the chief of the Vancouver [Police Department], briefed me on the system.

I always use the missing women's file as an example because there was a party place in Coquitlam, and the police knew about it. So if you had a sex trade worker who was at this party, and the Vancouver police had a missing person file, they might fax it out. Not very effective, and a high risk that no one would see it.

There was a case outside Merritt where the police officer did a random check in the early 2000s. He pulled over a man and let him go after, and two hours later the man had murdered his ex-spouse. Meanwhile there was a court order prohibiting him for being anywhere near Merritt.

Today, his name would be in the PRIME [Police Records Information Management Environment] system we set up, and the police officer would have known he was not permitted to be there, and there is a chance that the road check would have prevented the murder.

The thing that bugged me about that story is I really felt for the police officer. [I] think I did my job, and somebody died. It's a gut kick. He didn't know, but it's still an outcome.

Coleman, working with key police officers, was determined to set up a new communication program. This brought together the RCMP "E" Division (British Columbia) in a partnership with other municipal police agencies and the BC provincial government in a common information system.[97]

We decided to have an information system throughout BC where there would be real time communication. It's

97   Royal Canadian Mounted Police, Police Records Information
      Management Environment (PRIME-BC), Executive summary, 2005.

called PRIME and provides immediate integration of data through a combined data system.

Today, BC is the only place in North America where the police are all on the same system. Today, if someone went missing in Vancouver, it would be on every police officer's system throughout BC.

It sounds simple, but it wasn't. There were so many jurisdictions. The RCMP often think they are better than everyone else. Vancouver thinks they can do everything themselves, but they can't. It's a complicated culture.

The roadblock to this was the Commissioner of the RCMP for all of Canada named Giuliano Zaccardelli. There was never a bigger ass [of a] police officer. He was arrogant. He had his boots custom-made. The story is that he had other people polish his boots for him. He acted like royalty. When Bev became deputy, he thought food would be brought in, because he was used to having catered food brought in to his private boardroom. She said, 'No, we are going to the cafeteria.'

So I [said], 'I'm going to do PRIME.' I [went] through cabinet, I [went] through [the] Treasury Board. I knew if we said it's just a policy, the police [would] find a way around it. I said to cabinet, 'We have to make it the law. We have to force it to happen.'

I [got] all the chiefs on board in BC, most of the detachment leads, and I had Bev. The leaders of policing got this.

Then Zaccardelli [came] out here, he [had] lunch with the chief of Vancouver, the chief of Victoria, and others. The comment I got back was [he said] if this guy Coleman wants to do this, the RCMP want their own system. He was only a constable with us, what does he know? One of them looked at him and said, 'Have you met this guy?'

Then he met me. I had the Commissioner of the RCMP sitting in the room, and [he had] a tech guy sitting beside him, and Bev [was] nearby. I [could] see her face but they [couldn't].

Zaccardelli [went] into his pitch: The RCMP aren't going to do PRIME; we don't want other police forces having access to our data.

And I [said] to him, 'Well, Commissioner, BC is going to do PRIME—integration of information brings down barriers, it's intelligent, and the sharing of information is critical in dealing with and solving crime.'

He replie[d], 'I don't think we will do it. We are going to it our own way.'

It was a Tuesday, and I [said] to him, 'We are doing PRIME. The RCMP have a provincial contract, and I need to know you are going to do PRIME by 4:30 this afternoon.'

'What if we don't?'

'If you say no, that's fine with me. I will go to cabinet tomorrow morning and get permission from cabinet [to give] notice to the RCMP on their contract that we will no longer have the RCMP as our police force in British Columbia because you refuse to do PRIME.' Was it a bit of a bluff? Maybe, but he had to know I was dead serious.

Bev got this. She was smiling. She was a phenomenal leader. She understood and was on board.

About 4:25 we got the call that the RCMP would do PRIME. So we put legislation in the house and we brought it in across BC. That was probably the single biggest change to our system. There were a few bugs at first, but now it runs really well. Today the RCMP have a system across Canada [that] feeds into PRIME but... isn't integrated anywhere else outside BC.

Mike Morris was an RCMP officer who joined the force in 1973 and was in various detachments. He was in senior management in BC, went to Alberta, then returned and took over command of the north district of BC: 42 detachments, including a couple of airplanes and a 72-foot boat in Prince Rupert. Morris worked with Coleman after Morris became MLA in 2013. He met him when Coleman was solicitor general and Morris was the district officer, working on amalgamating a number of operational communication centres to the 911 system in northern BC, including Terrace, Prince George, Dawson Creek, and Prince Rupert. Morris wanted to centralize the system in Prince George, and technology had advanced enough that it could operate out of Prince George and not compromise public safety. The mayor of Dawson Creek at that time was a man named Blair Lekstrom.

Morris said, "I met with Coleman to discuss my plans, let him know what I was doing, and show how much money it would save, which was several million dollars. Blair opposed me, said he would oppose me every step of the way. Six families would lose jobs if the move was made to Prince George. I called my Commanding Officer and told her about the meeting. As I was driving back, my phone rang and it was Rich. He said, 'How did your meeting go?' so I told him. He said, 'Leave it with me, I will deal with Blair.'

"A day or so later I had a call from Blair and he told me he was on board."[98]

Coleman introduced another substantial change to policing systems. Called IHIT, which stands for Integrated Homicide Investigation Team, in 2024 it is the largest homicide unit in Canada, responsible for investigating homicides, suspicious deaths, and high-risk missing persons where foul play is suspected.[99] Coleman saw this as a bringing together of the best talent on the most challenging crimes. IHIT became a turnkey system with forensic specialists and other trained experts who could be assigned to cases.

"At first it was just RCMP because I could work well with Bev. The chief of Abbotsford was Ian McKenzie. I [got] a call from him: 'We want in. If you let us, I will send two people tomorrow, because this is murder insurance.' The Abbotsford Killer just about broke the local police force. His name was Terry Driver and the police had to dedicate resources, but they had no specialized resources.

"He attacked two girls with a baseball bat, killed one, then taunted the police with phone calls and letters to them for a while. The story started before I was elected. If there was a case like this again, you take 30 or 40 of your best officers and put them on the case."

The new system was quickly adopted and transformed response times to murders and other major crimes.

> The RCMP Integrated Homicide Investigation Team was put together with officers from Lower Mainland detachments such as Mission's and immediately responded to three killings.

---

98   Interview with Mike Morris, April 22, 2021, by Zoom.
99   Integrated Homicide Investigation Team, RCMP BC, https://bc-cb. rcmp-grc.gc.ca/ViewPage.action?siteNodeId=2139

"The Integrated Homicide Investigation Team has been up and running for a month now," outgoing team leader Sgt. Murray MacAulay of the RCMP Lower Mainland District said last week.

The IHIT caseload quickly increased to eight homicides and two attempted homicides by the end of its first month of operation, MacAulay said...

He attributes the team's initial success to the hard work of his team and the members in each of the jurisdictions they have been involved with.

He said, "This is definitely groundbreaking. This is an example of integration that's gone forward and is working." MacAulay said 46 of the most experienced investigators are dedicated to the team that investigates homicide and attempted homicide cases throughout anywhere from Pemberton and Boston Bar.[100]

Coleman gives a lot of credit to the bureaucrats who recommended the new programs. "I was the minister. I just took good advice. Kevin Begg, Director of Police Services, helped put the policy together. They would come to me and tell me what they needed for a specific case, like the Hells Angels house in Nanaimo. You couldn't talk about the investigation. It would jeopardize it. They could finally go to a minister and ask for the resources and get [them]."

IHIT has one of the best solve rates in North America because of this integration.

---

100 *Integrated murder team breaking new ground: [Final Edition]*, Kevin Gillies, *Abbotsford Times*, Abbotsford, BC, July 1, 2003.

Chapter 18
PICKTON AND THE PIG FARM

I believe if we had PRIME in the 1990s we would have caught him sooner and we would have saved lives. It was nobody's fault how that went—people said the police weren't paying attention to missing people, but they didn't have the system to share information. It was done by faxes to the offices. It wasn't in the car with the police officers. There was only so much paper they could carry.

—Rich Coleman[101]

In early 2002, I was doing final interviews for my book on former NDP Premier Glen Clark. He was going through a criminal trial and his lawyer was the articulate and effective litigator David Gibbons, assisted by Richard Fowler. In the same office was Peter Ritchie, a partner in the firm and at that time representing accused serial killer Robert Pickton.[102] Gibbons was generous with his time on the phone and invited me to his office at the Vancouver Marine Building near the waterfront, an iconic art deco historic

---

101 Interview with Rich Coleman, March 19, 2022, in person.
102 *Total tab for Clark prosecution, inquiry nears $4 million: Taxpayer on hook for staggering sums as cost of Crown lawyers, witnesses, police investigations comes to light in high-profile cases: [Final Edition]*, Neal Hall, *The Vancouver Sun*, Vancouver, BC, November 20, 2002.

tower, often the scene of Marvel comic movies today. His office was, as expected, rich in wood and beautifully set out. I waited a few minutes at reception for Gibbons to be available, and when I walked into his office he was visibly shaken. He apologized for making me wait and told me he needed a few minutes; he was helping to review evidence in the Pickton case. He paused for a moment and said, "I can't say anything specific, just don't eat pork chops from any pig farms anywhere near Port Coquitlam." Ritchie removed himself as the lawyer representing Pickton some time after that.

Robert Pickton was one of Canada's worst convicted serial killers and the case against him unfolded over years, with teams of investigators working through evidence and combing through the land and buildings of his pig farm, trying to piece together what happened and gather evidence to nail down the truth. There had been stories linking the missing women to the Pickton pig farm for years.

Why did it take so long for a formal investigation? What did they find when they went through the farm? Coleman was solicitor general and a former RCMP officer. He walked the grounds from the beginning and ensured the resources were available to handle the case as its size spiralled to record spending.

It was a complicated and horrific case, high-profile and emotional, and in 2004 BC Provincial Health Officer Dr. Perry Kendall publicly acknowledged that there were human remains mixed in with the pork, which sent shock waves through the country. The story came out only because of the potential health risk. In fact, the officers investigating the case had known for some time that human remains were being served as food.

The meat was distributed or sold to at least 40 relatives, friends, and associates of Pickton but was never sold in retail stores or made widely available to the public...

"As a result of information we received from the RCMP, we have reason to believe there is a strong possibility that some of the product from the Pickton farm, and how much the RCMP do not know, may still be sitting in some people's freezers in the Lower Mainland."

"We have an obligation to mitigate what may be a small public health risk, even though the meat is two years old and frozen. It would still have the capacity to carry the infection," Kendall said.

...He said some people known to have eaten or received meat from the property have already been contacted.[103]

Coleman became solicitor general in June of 2001, and the search of the property began on February 5, 2002. There had been attempts to follow up on tips about Pickton since 1998. The NDP created a Task Force for Missing Women in April 2001, but it did not have enough resources to deal with a case the size of the Pickton case. The jurisdictional issues between the RCMP and the Vancouver Police Department were an obstacle to proper investigation.

When the formal investigation began, Pickton and his siblings stated through their lawyer Peter Ritchie that they were shocked that the police were searching their farm. Pickton's statements at the beginning combined with the facts as they came out later show what a skilled and manipulative liar he was. The media were already aware something significant was underway; however, even then there was no confirmation that he was a person of interest in the missing women files. By the time the large-scale property search began, there were 65 missing women, most of them people

---

103 *Human remains feared in Pickton meat: [Final Edition]*, Amy O'Brian and Petti Fong, *The Vancouver Sun*, Vancouver, BC, March 11, 2004.

with substance use disorders and sex workers, marginalized and poor, and many of them Indigenous.

> On Friday, police refused to confirm if their painstaking search of Pickton's property has yielded the remains or personal possessions of any of the 50 women, some of whom have been missing since 1983.

> But Vancouver police Detective Scott Driemel told about 60 local, national and international media gathered for an afternoon news conference at a building supply store parking lot overlooking the farm that they are prepared to scour the entire 10-acre search area "inch by inch" in an investigation that may take months to complete.[104]

After doing the research on how Coleman managed systems and strategy in the public interest, applied his experience as an RCMP officer to his analysis, and worked with the best teams possible, it is clear to me that his approach to the Pickton case broke the log-jam. It is not a coincidence that within months of becoming solicitor general, he had deployed the resources, supported the investigative teams, and followed staff and investigators' advice to facilitate a strategy to nail Pickton. During the three-and-a-half years between the initial tips and the full-scale investigation that Coleman activated, more women were killed.

The murder trail led to Pickton years before the full investigation in 2002.

> Police received a tip in July, 1998, about Pickton, who had also been charged with the attempted murder of a

---

104 *Robert Pickton 'flabbergasted' by police search: Family is willing to 'assist police' as forensic digging begins at farm: [Final Edition],* Jeff Lee, Scott Simpson, and Neal Hall, *The Vancouver Sun,* Vancouver, BC, February 9, 2002.

Vancouver prostitute and other offences in March, 1997. The charges were later stayed.

Vancouver city police investigators later developed a second source pointing at Pickton, but it's unclear why it took three years for police to search his farm, which is in RCMP jurisdiction.

Sources have told The Sun there was a disagreement over the accuracy of some of the source information, and the investigation eventually stalled.

By late 2000, the Vancouver city police had already scaled back their investigation of the missing women case and were conducting a file review with the intention of asking the provincial unsolved homicide unit for further analysis.

A joint RCMP-Vancouver city police team then began reviewing the cases of all murdered and missing prostitutes in 2001, and the police have said it was during that file review that Pickton's name surfaced again.

Since the summer of 1998, 18 women—including Abotsway and Wilson—have disappeared from the Downtown Eastside.[105]

Coleman knew about the witness who initiated the 1998 investigation. He also knew that to get a conviction, you had to have a credible witness; someone who would withstand cross-examination. He took time to absorb the whole story she told in 1998, which was that she had been captured and taken to the

---

105 'Shocked' Pickton faces court: Alleged murder victims disappeared three years after police received tip about accused: [Final Edition], Kim Bolan and Lindsay Kines, The Vancouver Sun, Vancouver, BC, February 26, 2002.

pig farm, and that she had escaped. She told police that she had seen someone being cut up, and the police went to the farm with the best warrant they could get, which allowed them to search for about an hour. They did not find anything. Then the jurisdictional issues between the Vancouver police, who were receiving the tips, and the RCMP, who had jurisdiction over the farm, made it very difficult to follow up. Coleman was bothered by the lack of progress and informed his staff he wanted to be kept up to date on all the information as they received it. Twenty years later, he still cannot reveal all the information he had to review. The interview about this file demonstrated how deeply it affected him. He walked the road with the police, forensic workers, and staff who had to go through the details of the case to get to conviction, and he knows they all paid a price with their mental health.

Kevin Begg calls me and says, 'I think we found him, but the warrant doesn't go far enough, so we are suspending the search and going for a wider warrant.' They had found some of the possessions of the missing women, so they thought they had something.

At the first briefing, I asked, 'What have you got?' It was almost sensory overload because you're not on the site, you're just being briefed. They said, 'We suspect he was mixing human remains with the ground pork,' and they were right. I don't know how they figured that out.

Begg said, 'This is going to be expensive.' The number was $15 million, so I had to go to finance, which was Gary Collins, and I said, 'It's for the investigation of the missing women. I can't tell you what it's for specifically. We have a breakthrough, and if we are right then that's just the start of the cost.'

He said, 'Fine.' The finance minister can do what is called a Treasury Board minor—it gets reported out later to Treasury Board. He used his spending authority. So I met with Kevin and I asked how much he needed. PRIME wasn't up and running yet. It had nothing to do with getting lucky on this one.

They expanded the search and it became apparent they had some human remains. Toughest part of being solicitor general. There are files I can't even talk about today, but I had to be briefed on them.[106]

Coleman watched as the investigation became more complicated. They were all certain that the murderer was Pickton, and they also knew there were many family members of the victims who were looking for closure. The culture of the investigation was one of respect for the missing women. Coleman and the team wanted to set a tone that made them a priority and let the public know that while they may have been marginalized members of society, there would be resources available to ensure that the best job was done to find every missing person who had been murdered on the farm.

The farm's acreage was sifted thoroughly, and there were archeological students brought in from UBC to see if there were teeth or bones left anywhere. They took care to check the land, see if there were remains buried. Then there was the investigation that had to be conducted inside the buildings, where the murders had taken place.

"I toured the site twice. I saw people in white coats, and I was there to get an understanding of the scope and size. I knew I would have to go and get the money." He paused and said with real emphasis, "I didn't want to contaminate the site and I didn't

106 Interview with Rich Coleman, March 19, 2022, in person.

want to see what was in the freezers." When Coleman was recalling the investigation, it was obvious that so many of the details were still very clear to him. "The land had to be searched carefully. We didn't find all the women." He spoke with the heaviness of grief 20 years later. "I visited the site a number of times, talked to the officers, those who were on the investigation. We knew we had the guy and we hadn't even gotten to the freezers yet. The freezers had meat and some body parts in them."

There were 90,000 DNA tests and thousands of exhibits to support the investigation and conviction.

Coleman absorbed the same information that his staff did. It was absolutely horrifying. Pickton was not the only one involved; however, the evidence did not reveal who else helped him. He was the one who was there every time. As for the remains after they murdered the women? "They fed them to the pigs. He mixed human remains in with his pork, ground pork and ground human. Most of this he gave to friends and people nearby. The Pickton investigation changed the perception of serial killers forever for everybody. I had a few books on serial killers trying to understand it.

"If you look at the history of serial killers, they have patterns, for example the Green River killer dropped the bodies beside the Green River. They operate in the disenfranchised communities like sex trade workers and the gay community. If you look a population of a few million people, the data suggests that there are two or three operating at any given time."

Pickton was often portrayed in the media as a simple, friendly man.

My eldest son, who is 25 years old, says, "Dad, Dad, did you hear? Uncle Willy, he's charged for murder."

At first, (Crisanto) Diopita didn't believe it. But then he watched the late news Friday and there it was: Robert

William Pickton, 52, charged with the first-degree murders of two of Vancouver's 50 missing women, all of whom were involved in drugs or the sex trade on the Downtown Eastside ..."He's a Workaholic"... "He's a very good guy."[107]

Coleman and his team took time to understand Pickton's serial killer pattern as part of the psychology of the investigation. "He had parties at his place. We assume he killed them then, but this time there were no bodies." An investigation without bodies was particularly challenging. How can such a simple, friendly man plan his murders so that all the body parts disappear? Clearly, Pickton was fully aware of what he was doing and was sure he could continue to escape capture as long as there was no evidence.

One reason the investigation was so expensive is that there were so many missing women, and the evidence had to be sorted in a lab.

"It was probably the first case solved by DNA." Coleman explained, "During the DNA process, we learned how to separate out human and animal DNA. We had to leave the meat and the bodies frozen, and they would take core samples, and then they would do the DNA tests on the core samples. The investigators on this were so good. The site was so organized, and the people on the case did a remarkable job, but the $15 million didn't last very long. In my time it was the most significant murder investigation in BC history. The only comparable one would have been Clifford Olsen. With Pickton you had a massive site, then there was another property... called Piggy's Palace and that's where the parties were. He would lure them to the farm somehow and then he would kill them."

By 2004, the headlines in the paper made it clear that $70 million had already been spent trying to solve the case. There were people who wanted to blame someone for spending so much

107 *Hog-raising Uncle Willy called an unlikely murder suspect*, Kim Bolan, Lindsay Kines, and Chad Skelton, *The Gazette*, Montreal, QC, February 25, 2002.

money and continuing the investigation when they had already charged Pickton. Coleman thought that by the time the case was over, the cost of investigation and prosecution was probably closer to $100 million. He saw this as the price that had to be paid to do the job right. Meanwhile, he would meet with family members during the entire process, and while he was compassionate and would hear them out, he could not share information that might compromise the investigation or the prosecution.

Vancouver city police media liaison Detective Scott Driemel said police will not comment on the investigation of Robert Pickton until after the courts have dealt with the matter.

"From what I understand about it, I'd have no problem explaining and discussing it with you; I think there's a ton of misinformation that's out there," Driemel said.

"If you armchair it and quarterback it now, is there things we could have done or should have done or might have done more of? It's pretty hard to put today's judgment on an issue that was there yesterday.

"But from what I've seen, it looks like we were reasonably diligent as far as how we dealt with the issues with the resources that we had available and how it unfolded."[108]

Coleman concluded his comments to me without looking at any notes. He has these facts etched into his memory. "I don't think we will ever know all the details... The police closed the case, and for everyone's sake we want to keep what we learned about it and move on and not think about it. There were people

---

108 Kim Bolan, Lindsay Kines, and Chad Skelton, ibid.

who were on that site for a year, I wouldn't be surprised if they had mental trauma.

"Robert Pickton was arrested February 22, 2002, convicted in 2007 on 6 counts, with 20 other counts stayed. He confessed to 49 murders to an officer undercover and may have been responsible for up to 60. He was one of the most prolific killers in Canadian history. He began the murders in the early 1980s after inheriting the pig farm. We tried to bring the families closure by handing them back the remains."

Chapter 19
WILDFIRES

KELOWNA, B.C. - Weary firefighters battled frustration as well as the Okanagan Mountain Park inferno that forced more evacuations Sunday and devoured more B.C. history. "You just have to look at it and go on," said Kirk Hughes, a fire information officer with the B.C. Forest Service. "We have to take the losses in stride and get back on the job the next day."

...On Saturday night, the winds led top officials to issue an extreme fire behaviour warning to their crews—ordering firefighters to conduct limited fire suppression only when it was safe to do so.[109]

—The Standard, September 2003

In 2003, Solicitor General Rich Coleman oversaw the first province-wide state of emergency in history, caused by a record series of wildfires. It started at the end of July and ran through August. It required fast action, strategic planning, immediate incident response, and a historic deployment of resources.

Coleman and his wife Michele were in Edmonton, heading to Calgary for a wedding, when he received a call from his deputy minister briefing him on the situation in the interior and

---

109 *Kelowna firefighters battle flames along with frustration: [Final Edition],*
The Standard, St. Catharines, ON, September 8, 2003.

providing him options— including calling a state of emergency to provide extraordinary powers that would allow him to move the resources around to where they were needed the most with no bureaucratic obstacles. Coleman had to go to the RCMP "E" Division headquarters in Edmonton to receive the paperwork, which he signed and sent back by fax. He then told Michele to go on to Calgary without him, and he headed back to Vancouver.

"I was able to take control of all fire services in BC. I was able to work with municipalities. For example, if we needed a fire truck in the south Okanagan, I could move a Surrey fire truck there and have Surrey's neighbour be prepared to back up Surrey's needs. It's a triage of the use of equipment. The situation continued to escalate and at one time we had 1,000 military providing support. Brought in equipment and moved firefighters around, including from the volunteer fire departments, which exist around BC to strategically backfill the province's resources."

Coleman spent a month talking to people and working on the ground, visiting local emergency centres, seeing the most effective use of resources. Controlling communication was also part of the management system he established.

"The media were banned, and we set up a structure for daily briefings from emergency workers. Later we allowed media in to look at the aftereffects of the Louis Creek fire which spread north into Barriere. They lost the Tolko Mill there."

The news stories were national, and as intense as the emergency, with many people sharing stories of loss. Thousands of people were evacuated, hundreds of homes were lost, and the fires were raging throughout the province, carried by high winds through extremely dry landscapes.

In ordering expansion of the state of emergency, Campbell said there now were 353 active fires in the province, including 25 new ones ignited in the 24 hours between Friday and Saturday afternoons. These fires had torched a total of 380 square kilometres...

B.C. Solicitor General Rich Coleman, in charge of the Provincial Emergency Program, would not rule out disaster assistance for Barriere residents, adding Ottawa had been informed of the request. But he said they will have to see just how bad the town has been hit.

The impact of British Columbia's summer of flame so far easily eclipses the most recent bad year – 1998.[110]

The evacuations kept expanding throughout the southern interior of the province, and the resources were targeted on where they were needed most—although even then, the people on the front line were getting tired.

Wildfires that have forced more than 10,000 southern B.C. residents from their homes are rapidly growing despite efforts from hard-pressed firefighters, officials said Sunday.

Although firefighters have made progress in specific areas, new thermal images and calculations show that three major fires in the Kamloops area have expanded and the six-day forecast is predicting more dry, hot weather.

The latest estimates of the McLure-Barriere fire, about 50 kilometres north of Kamloops, found it had spread by almost 30 per cent compared with Saturday's estimates, now covering more than 84 square kilometres.[111]

---

110 *B.C.'s worst fire season in 5 decades forces more than 10,000 from homes,* Carol Harrington, *Canadian Press NewsWire,* Toronto, ON, August 3, 2003.
111 *Major B.C. wildfires rapidly growing, forcing more residents to flee homes,* Carol Harrington, *Canadian Press NewsWire,* Toronto, ON, August 3, 2003.

Coleman responded to the unprecedented fires by creating a new central agency that could go beyond the State of Emergency with a planned response and integrated resources. This new department was created and activated within days and had sweeping powers to order local firefighters onto the front line to boost the efforts by the provincial and federal people fighting the fires. At the time that Coleman created this new department, there were over 850 wildfires burning.

"The situation in our province this summer goes beyond anything we have experienced in the past," Coleman said.

The province's fire commissioner will now be able to pull firefighters and equipment from any jurisdiction within B.C. to fight wildfires. Coleman said the new department, established under the Emergency Program Act, starts immediately.

The central and southeast regions are in greatest immediate danger, and the provincial force will have regional departments in place in Cranbrook and Kamloops, each with a regional chief and district chiefs.

Local fire chiefs will remain in command of their areas. But if they need extra help, they will turn to the regional office of the provincial force, which has the power to bring in equipment and crews from other areas.

Provincial fire commissioner Rick Dumala said the new measures are unprecedented. "This is the first jurisdiction in North America to set up such a co-ordinated firefighting effort to meet emergency response needs," he said.

The announcement comes more than two years after the province's auditor general warned of inadequate preparations for wildfires, and criticized the lack of a single agency to direct the response ...

Auditor General Wayne Strelioff was critical of a lack of preparation in high-risk areas and confusion about responsibilities of local and provincial governments. Strelioff also warned that a build-up of combustible materials after years of successful fire suppression was creating the risk of major fires propelled by large amounts of fuel.[112]

In the midst of all of this, the Kelowna fire occurred. It was a fire on a scale that few had experienced, and it was near the largest populated city in the BC interior, in the middle of the Okanagan Valley. I am from Kelowna. It's where I was elected as an MLA, and my daughters, youngest sister, aunts, and cousins were all living in Kelowna at that time, plus many friends. So the fire in Okanagan Mountain Park was immediately a huge concern. I knew that the breeze blowing off the lake could run the fire along the south slopes, and my aunt Munira Murrey lived very close to Okanagan Mountain Park. I watched anxiously as the fire continued to grow.

Premier Gordon Campbell and Prime Minister Jean Chrétien came to Kelowna to provide support and be directly informed of the situation. Prime Minister Chrétien was very familiar with that part of Kelowna since Senator Ross Fitzpatrick, his long-time friend, owned a winery called Cedar Creek at the end of Lakeshore Road, close to Okanagan Mountain Park.

Coleman remembers, "It was the largest evacuation in BC history, about 30,000 people evacuated, and we flew over in a helicopter. The greatest picture never taken was when Campbell and Chrétien were getting into one helicopter. I'm getting into

---

112 *New provincial fire department to tackle wildfires: Drastic measures required says Coleman, so powerful department created: [Final Edition]*, Paul Willcocks, *Nelson Daily News*, Nelson, BC, August 20, 2003.

the other one and I missed a step, did a face plant on the ground. Would have looked like a bumbling idiot, but no one was paying attention to me. Prime Minister joked with me afterward, 'Hey, you had a pretty bad fall! Good thing it was you—if it was me, it would have been the national news.'"

Coleman had to make some very difficult decisions about how to manage the fire because it was so strong and posed an enormous threat. It was all about mitigating risk and trying to anticipate what would happen next in a situation that was evolving constantly.

"We were working under extraordinary powers that day. We flew into Penticton because the smoke in Kelowna was too bad. He asked me what I thought and I said the morning was fine, but the afternoons are always windy. I had made the decision that at 5:00 p.m. that day we were going to bulldoze about ten houses' worth, around 400 to 500,000 each. But then we couldn't get up there with the heavy equipment because of all the people parked to watch the fire, so we lost the whole subdivision.

"I had told Campbell that we were going to do it about a quarter to six. Said don't tell anyone, but as premier you should know, so he did an interview and kept calm. Later that night the whole thing went down."

The headlines about the Kelowna fire help provide some context.

Inferno races toward Kelowna: Fires force more to flee in Okanagan, Sun Peaks[113]

Scorched regions shock premier[114]

---

113 *Inferno races toward Kelowna: Fires force more to flee in Okanagan, Sun Peaks: [Final Edition]*, Amy O'Brian, *Times-Colonist*, Victoria, BC, September 8, 2003.

114 *Scorched regions shock premier: [Final Edition]*, Carol Harrington, *Trail Times*, Trail, BC, August 6, 2003.

B.C. forest fires force more evacuations: 4,000 people in Kelowna are out of their homes[115]

B.C. issues backcountry travel ban[116]

Coleman continued to maintain his cool and stayed directly in touch with people on the ground. He took time to visit the emergency operations centres and fire centres; to talk to the people in charge and understand what was needed; and to speak with the evacuees and people who had lost their homes to help create a plan. He felt that his job was to put his own plans aside, like a friend's wedding and a summer holiday, and show up for the people who needed him.

"It isn't about fixing things; it's about showing that someone gives a damn. In 2004, I was beat up in public accounts for the amount of pizza I bought, saying it was irresponsible to spend that much money on pizza. I finally said to the reporter who went on about it that I bought it for the firefighters who had worked 12-hour days fighting fires."

In the 2003 year-end summary, Brian Hutchinson of the *National Post* provided this perspective:

> It was chaos and control, all at once. The wildfires did not arrive unannounced, but they came quickly, with staggering force. We were prepared; we were ill-prepared. Plans were followed and plans were ignored. Things went smoothly; things went awry.
>
> This is what happens in a natural disaster. Humans become confused and helpless, heroic and strong. Emotions build

---

115 *B.C. forest fires force more evacuations: 4,000 people in Kelowna are out of their homes: [Final Edition], Observer,* Sarnia, ON, September 8, 2003.

116 *B.C. issues backcountry travel ban: [Final Edition],* Matthew Ramsey, *The Ottawa Citizen,* Ottawa, ON, August 29, 2003.

and explode and we are, somehow, transformed. We become less naive, more wary, but we remain the same. Everything is different, yet nothing has really changed.

The fires that razed the B.C. interior this summer left behind ugly, toxic scars. First hit was the little town of Barriere; next came Kelowna, an affluent, arid paradise sandwiched between Okanagan Lake and a tinder-dry mountain forest. In the end, hundreds of houses were gone, their entire contents incinerated. Heirlooms were turned to ash. Memories were erased. Thousands of people were forced to find emergency shelter in hockey arenas, in hotel rooms or with friends and relatives.

The fires were terrifying, but awesome. Almost exquisite. They assaulted the senses. They roared. Flames leaped from one treetop to the next, creating a stunning visual effect known as "candling." And the smell: It was good, like a campfire.[117]

My aunt Munira Murrey lost her home and our family lost most of our treasured home movies and photos from India in the Okanagan Mountain Fire. Our family joined hundreds of others in that fire, and many in the years to come, in having a story like this. The gratitude for the saving of lives is what remains, and for many of us, 2003 was the beginning of the new reality in BC called "wildfire season"—which now, in 2024, is an annual time of year.

---

117 *That fearsome roar: [National Edition]*, Brian Hutchinson, *National Post*, Toronto, ON, December 27, 2003.

Housing advocacy

Housing and Social Development Minister Rich Coleman addresses a study session on making homeownership more affordable in B.C. in 2010.

At the Union of BC Municipalities convention in 2016, Housing Minister Coleman addresses a session on Tent Cities and Homelessness.

Digging in on housing funding

In 2011, kindergarten students Avery and Kaitlyn break ground on
the Lynn Fripps Elementary School (left to right): Langley Education Board Chair
Steve Burton; Township of Langley Mayor Rick Green; MLA Rich Coleman;
Simon vander Goes, husband of Lynn Fripps, Education Minister George Abbott.

In 2012, a new housing and youth centre breaks ground in Vancouver.
(Left to right) Vancouver Mayor Gregor Robertson, Caroline Bonesky,
Family Services, Rich Coleman, Mary McNeil, Minister of Children and
Family Development, Nancy Keough, Kettle Friendship Society;
and Geoff Plant, Steettohome Foundation.

In 2015 a $29.3M investment for affordable housing for seniors in Burnaby at Derby Manor. Burnaby North MLA Richard T. Lee, Derek Corrigan, Burnaby Mayor, Joanne Reid, board chair, George Derby Care Society.

Resource projects

July of 2011 at the Waneta Dam expansion construction project near Trail. The dam provides enough clean energy to power 60,000 homes per year and reduces greenhouse gas emissions by 400,000 tonnes.

2011 Copper Mountain is the first new major metals mine since 199. From left: Copper Mountain CEO Jim O'Rourke, Mining Association of BC President Karina Brino, Rich Coleman, Princeton Mayor Randy McLean, Pierre Gratton, Mining Association of Canada President, and Penticton MLA Barisoff.

In 2013 at a tour of northern LNG sites hosted by Shell, with Deputy Minister Brian Hansen and Oil and Gas Commissioner Paul Jeakins.

November 2012 the Nisga'a Nation and province sign a benefits agreement for the Prince Rupert Gas Transmission Pipeline. Right to left: Rich Coleman, Minister of Aboriginal Relations and Reconciliation John Rustad, and President of the Nisga'a Nation Mitchell Stevens.

The Advent of LNG in BC

April 2014 Premier Christy Clark and Rich Coleman witness the signing of a joint venture agreement for a proposed liquefied natural gas (LNG) export project with representatives from Shell, PetroChina, LNG Canada, Mitsubishi and KOGAS.

Speaking at the 2014 Trade Mission to Kuala Lumpur
about the opportunities in BC, especially LNG.

Touring the Petronas LNG complex as part of the 2014 Trade Mission in Bintulu,
Saraka. It comprises three LNG plans with a capacity of 23 million tons per
annum making it the world's largest LNG production facility on a single site.

First Nations engagement

In 2014, the Government of BC signs a revenue sharing agreement with the Lax Kw'alaams and Metlakatla First Nations to develop LNG export facilities at Grassy Point near Prince Rupert. Left to right, front to back: Rich Coleman, Alrita Leask, John Rustad, Chief Harold Leighton, Premier Christy Clark.

Minister of Natural Gas Development Rich Coleman and Lax Kw'alaams Mayor John Helin chat on their way to a briefing by PETRONAS in the fall of 2016.

In 2017, Lax Kw'alaams Mayor John Helin, Premier Christy Clark, and Minister Rich Coleman are working together on the LNG project.

Housing policy and community engagement

In 2014, Canada and BC extend affordable housing funding, with Minister of State Candice Bergen signing the expansion in funding.

In 2015, Coleman celebrates the opening of the social housing in Vancouver with BC Housing CEO Shayne Ramsay, Minister Rich Coleman and Councillor Kerry Jang, City of Vancouver.

In 2015 Paul Nichols, a resident of Kersley, BC and a veteran of the Canadian Armed Forces, led a band of fellow veterans on an 11,000 km eight-month horseback ride across Canada starting from the front steps of the BC legislature.

June 2016, federal, provincial and territorial ministers responsible for housing met to discuss key priorities for housing in Canada, including a National Housing Strategy and with a long term vision to meet the housing needs of Canadians.

2017 at Backyard Vineyards in Langley, five Fraser Valley agrifood companies came together as recipients of Buy Local funding. Langley MLA Mary Polak, Fort Langley-Aldergrove MLA Rich Coleman and Chilliwack MLA John Martin joined Backyard Vineyards, Dead Frog Brewery, Vista D'Oro Farms, Fraser Valley Specialty Poultry and Gojoy Berries to learn more about the local foods British Columbians are eating.

February 2017 Coleman appointed the Building Officials' Association of British Columbia (BOABC) as the administrative authority for qualification requirements for local government building. (L to R) Manjit Sohi, President, BOABC, Rich Coleman, Ron Dickinson, Past President, BOABC, Derek Townson, Executive Director, BOABC.

Deputy Premier and Cabinet

In September of 2012 Premier Clark presents new cabinet heading into 2013 election. Back row (L-R): Michael de Jong, Don McRae, Bill Bennett, Margaret MacDiarmid, John Yap, Rich Coleman, Steve Thomson, Mary Polak, Naomi Yamamoto, Terry Lake, Shirley Bond, Pat Bell. Front row (L-R): Ralph Sultan, Ida Chong, Moira Stilwell, Premier Christy Clark, the Honourable Steven Point, Lieutenant Governor, Norm Letnick, Ben Stewart, Stephanie Cadieux.

In September 2013 Premier Clark meets with her cabinet ministers after her election victory in the Okanagan.

Family

Michele Coleman and the grandchildren sing at
the annual Coleman community BBQ in Langley.

Rich and Michele visit with constituents and guests at the annual BBQ.

Coleman addresses his constituents and guests
at the annual community BBQ.

Chapter 20
FARMING TO FORESTRY

> *"My mind," he said, "rebels at stagnation. Give me problems, give me work, give me the most abstruse cryptogram or the most intricate analysis, and I am in my own proper atmosphere. I can dispense then with artificial stimulants. But I abhor the dull routine of existence. I crave for mental exaltation…"*
>
> —Sherlock Holmes, *The Sign of the Four*, by Sir Arthur Conan Doyle

Coleman enjoyed being at the table to discuss problems, listen to input, and provide feedback. Sometimes he was able to solve a problem outside his direct portfolio, if the scale of the problem had made it part of his responsibilities.

In 2004 an agriculture problem on the farms in the Fraser Valley escalated to the point that he had to get involved. It was an outbreak of Avian flu, and it was devastating the chicken farmers. It took weeks for the tragedy to get under control.

> Avian flu has been virtually stamped out in B.C.'s Fraser Valley, emergency officials said Thursday, leaving empty barns and destitute farmers in its wake.

There is simply no more fuel to spread the virus, now that crews have completed the cull of 1.3 million birds on 42 infected properties. More than 15 million more were ordered slaughtered after testing negative and then processed for human consumption...

Kiley said 10 per cent of the chickens in the valley remain untouched, and will be spared as long as there is no further spread. Those birds are owned mostly by breeder operations in Chilliwack, located in the eastern region of the Fraser Valley where no infection was ever detected.

He said most of the 600 backyard flocks in the area have been killed off, but expects investigators may find more small holdings as they criss-cross the region. Those operations will immediately be depopulated as well.[118]

After the birds were killed, there was the problem of disposing of them without the risk of further contamination. It was a very cumbersome, expensive process. Coleman remembers the time well, and that there were meetings being held to try to sort out what to do with the millions and millions of culled chickens. "We were sending them to an old mine in Princeton. We were burning the chickens in the mine, but this thing was spreading. It was in the feed. We needed to burn them and had to get the fire hot enough to kill the virus. Jon Van Dongen was the minister of agriculture. I was sent in by Campbell on emergency measures stuff, so I was talking to the farmers. Out of the blue, I asked them, 'How hot does it get inside an ag bag, where you put stuff to compost?' They replied that it gets pretty hot, so I asked the staff to find out how hot and said that we needed to put all the feed and all the chickens into ag bags."

118 *Cull complete, bird flu under control: official,* Amy Carmichael, *Prince George Citizen,* Prince George, BC, May 28, 2004.

Coleman knew from his past time around farms that if the temperature became hot enough, they could put everything into composting bags, sometimes called ag bags or silo bags, dispose of them into a compost, and six months later have topsoil free of the virus. The bags also contained any smell or possible contamination of the air or soil during the composting process.

"For days I had sat around with scientists trying to solve this because it was so serious. In order to save the remaining chickens, we needed to stop the disease from crossing the Vedder Canal. We found out the bags became hot enough. It was a practical answer to the problem. I never said to anyone I came up with this idea of ag bags."

Vaughn Palmer summed up Coleman's work as solicitor general in the 16 years that the BC Liberals were in government. "I lost track of the number of times he was solicitor general. Every time they got rid of one, Rich came back."[119]

The first time Coleman moved out of the position of solicitor general was in 2005. He was called in to meet Gordon Campbell on a Saturday and told he would be the next minister of health. Coleman immediately called Deputy Minister of Health Penny Ballam to ask what he needed to know.

"For a week, I was going to be the health minister. Then I get a phone call from Campbell on Friday, meet him the next day, and he tells me he wants me to move to a resource file and gives me minister of forests. I didn't want to go—your first ministry is your first love—and I wasn't going to be the forests minister, I was going to be the health minister." Coleman had already started working on a new model for health information systems, and he was disappointed. He soon overcame his disappointment and turned his attention to his first ministry.

On June 16, 2005, Rich Coleman became minister of forests and range, and minister responsible for housing. At that time, housing

---

119 Interview with Vaughn Palmer, December 6, 2023, by Zoom.

was not a stand-alone ministry; it was simply an add-on responsibility. In his list of general responsibilities, he had forest stewardship and timber supply; forest protection (pests and fire), compliance, and enforcement; forest investment; timber pricing and sales; BC timber sales; grazing and range stewardship; and housing and homelessness policy. In addition, he took over the following major agencies, boards, and commissions: Forest Appeals Commission, Forest Practices Board, Forestry Innovation Investments Ltd., Timber Export Advisory Committee, BC Housing Management Commission, and Premier's Taskforce on Homelessness.

"When I was in opposition, I had toured a bunch of mills as deputy forests critic. I had been through the Kootenays with David Gray, who was someone working in forestry for years. He knew every mill and understood the industry. I learned a lot. So now I'm forests minister and the first thing I did was meet every CEO I could of every forest company.

"One meeting was up in Hundred Mile House and I asked if they could feed me all the information I need[ed] in order to do a good job. The older guy said, 'This is a different experience for us. Do you know, we have never met with a minister or had anyone from government come to talk to us?'"

Coleman developed a personal connection with many of the business owners and took time to talk to them about their experiences and perspectives. He toured a variety of operations, from primary extraction to value-added, and absorbed the information.

"You find out about the technology. It's incredible to learn from the people running the businesses. In one operation, there was a saw that could cut through the logs using a laser and straighten out some of the kinks which provided added value to the logs by creating more dimensional lumber. The whole system is fascinating.

"One of the greatest opportunities an MLA has is to show up at any mill, mine, [or] dam and... be welcomed by the people who are doing the jobs. You won't learn anything sitting in your office."[120]

One of the biggest challenges for the Canadian forest sector was trying to reach a legal agreement with the United States on what is called softwood lumber. The softwood lumber industry is and always has been a key industry in BC and across Canada. In 2005 it was putting $2 billion into our economy. Coleman took control of the file as minister and set a goal of reaching an agreement, which had never been done before.

Coleman explained the basics of the issue. "The industry kept going to court trying to get free trade. This issue had been around since the 1970s. There had been hybrid deals. The US kept trying to slap on duties—they didn't want to compete with us; they thought we had an uneven playing field because of Crown land. The reality is that the US is actually the protectionist in this deal.

"We absolutely have to have access to the US market. They were 85% of our market. That is slowly changing, but without the US market, our softwood industry cannot succeed. They were crippling us with duties and countervailing duties at the border, and when they slapped the duties and countervailing duties on us, [those] funds [were] put into trust in the US because of all the litigation. Our industry had to pay the duties if they wanted to sell their lumber."

Coleman read through the existing documents on the file. He saw a path toward a Softwood Lumber Agreement. "I flew to Alberta, Saskatchewan, and Ontario, met the Quebec minister... and said we are going to lead [the softwood lumber talks] because BC is the biggest player. They agreed to work with me. Alberta was with us right away. I said, 'This is our oil' and they got it right away. I told everyone else if it gets too complicated, we will never get a deal."

---

120 Interview with Rich Coleman, March 19, 2022, in person.

David Emerson was the federal minister of forests at that time and was very supportive of Coleman's efforts. Emerson was from British Columbia and had spent most of his career in the forest industry. Coleman spent time in Ottawa working with Emerson and went to Washington to meet with Michael Wilson, our ambassador to the United States.

"I did the groundwork before I went, found out that in the past when we wanted to talk softwood lumber, a delegation... made up of the big companies and their lawyers [would go], and in theory they were working together, but in reality every company had its own agenda. So before I met with Michael, I talked to many of the players, which also included the small- and medium-sized businesses, and I decided we were not going to try to conclude a softwood lumber deal by going to Washington. We were going to coordinate everything in BC. We were going to bring everyone together and create the consensus.

"I basically lived at the Sheraton Wall and created a war room for about four weeks. We had whiteboards; we held conferences. I called players together. We were just buried in the topic. It was totally consuming for a few weeks. I went between the players, working to create consensus between the big players on a deal that would work for the smaller players. There was always this tension as I tried to broker something everyone could agree to sign."

In my years in politics, I had a chance to meet many of the key players in the forest sector, and I knew enough about the softwood lumber issue to know that it was and is massively complicated, with very high stakes and a lot of "alpha male" energy in the room when the discussions were underway. Coleman knew that he had to reach an agreement and that the fundamentals had to be condensed to two pages. He knew he could do that. He also wanted all the duties that had been paid to be repaid to the industry, and he wanted to stop paying them as part of the agreement.

"BC was always the target of the US duties, because we were

the biggest. The US would fight us because they didn't want to compete with us. We could beat them on price [and] production, and we were good at producing lumber. We had the most modern systems and the best structure. They had private land and old mills. The lumber trade council in the US was a huge lobby with Congress on their side, [and] they would keep trying to drive us down. You look at the duties and it's stunning.

"I needed to focus people. If you give people a hundred options, you will never get focus because there will always be something to fight over. You need an outline of where the deal can go. The guys in Ontario and Quebec have mills that are not very efficient or competitive. They just wanted quota of what they could cut and deliver to the US. The quota system is not a good economic model for lumber, and it would not have worked for BC anyway.

"We ended up with a compromise where we had two options to present to the provincial governments and they could opt in to one or the other. Either Option A, which was a form of freer trade based on volume, which worked for everyone except Ontario and Quebec, or Option B, a quota system, which is what Ontario and Quebec chose. The volume-based model had pricing and other elements baked in to it.[121]

Over the decades there were other deals, but none that represented a successful ten-year Softwood Lumber Agreement. Coleman felt that the key was to make sure there was a deal that could get buy-in from the whole country of Canada, sign the major companies up to that model, and then make sure the model could accommodate the smaller players. That way, before sitting down with the United States, there would be a uniform voice across Canada, in the public and private sectors, speaking on behalf of all Canadian interests.

Coleman remembers, "It was a very intense four weeks in Vancouver. The deal was agreed to and signed in April 2006. Took

---

121 Interview with Rich Coleman, March 19, 2022, in person.

me less than a year, although it felt longer. When you get people on the same page, you can get things done."

The deal was a high-profile, national story, and there was a lot of talk in the mainstream media and the trade journals about it. The coverage was generally positive. It was a ten-year agreement.

> U.S. Ambassador David Wilkins yesterday called the softwood lumber deal the proof that Canada matters in Washington, and the precursor of a new era of co-operation between the two countries.

> "Leadership matters," he told a Public Policy Forum conference in Ottawa. "Call it a breath of fresh air, a new effort, new energy, a renewed momentum, whatever term you want to describe it - but there is a sense, in my opinion, both in Washington and in Ottawa, that we are entering a positive, productive stage in our relationship."

> The deal announced on Thursday gives Canada free access to the U.S. market, provided lumber prices remain at their current high level. The U.S. also agreed to return $4 billion of the $5.3 billion (U.S.) in tariffs that it has imposed during this latest dispute over softwood lumber.

> But for some, the deal is reminiscent of the situation that existed before 1995 when Canada broke the existing managed trade arrangement.

> "That's a fair observation - but there are differences," Gary Huffbauer of the Washington-based Institute for International Economics told the Star. "People do learn from experience - and this is a more market-friendly arrangement."

Huffbauer, who is a critic of managed trade and a supporter of free trade, told the conference that the new deal represented managed trade, not free trade.

"We're not fans of managed trade, but managed trade is better than a trade war, especially one that soured the whole (Canada–U.S.) relationship," he said. "It's a definite improvement."[122]

Coleman had spent four solid weeks working out of a hotel on the agreement, and when the deal was done, it was time for the "lights, camera, action" of politics so there could be some political benefit for all the hard work. His home was in Langley, at least an hour in the direction away from the airport, and in politics, timing is everything. He had to improvise. "Essentially what happened [was] we did a deal, I think it was [on] a Tuesday, [and] I had to go cabinet so I flew to Victoria. I didn't have a suitcase on me. I had consensus, and now I knew I needed to get it approved by cabinet. I got it through cabinet, and then some of my colleagues helped by calling individual companies [to] make sure they were on board."

The deal was recognized as helpful even on the East Coast.

The Maritime Lumber Bureau is cheering the new Canada–U.S. softwood lumber deal.

"We believe this is a good day and a good announcement," Maritime Lumber Bureau President Diana Blenkhorn said in a telephone conference with reporters.

---

122 *U.S. hails new era after deal; Envoy touts co-operation with Canada But some see old practices in place: [Ontario Edition]*, Graham Fraser, *Toronto Star*, Toronto, ON, April 29, 2006.

"It is a fair agreement" that "recognizes the innocence of Atlantic Canada."

Blenkhorn said the new agreement exempts the east coast firms from the tariff schedule that will take effect should the price of lumber fall, and that the region's exports will not be subject to a quota.

About 100 east coast lumber companies are in line to get 80 per cent of the $130-million in duties they have paid the U.S. treasury over the past five years.[123]

"We worked it," Coleman said. "I was exhausted, and there was a joint cabinet meeting in Alberta later the same day. I had no change of clothes, nothing, but I'm getting on a plane to Alberta and there was no time to grab anything." Fortunately, there are ways to manage to look good in a suit even if it's the same one for a week straight. Coleman recalls that the cabinet secretary Elizabeth McMillan saw that he had arrived without anything for travel, so she found him all the basics, plus a clean shirt.

Coleman briefed all the cabinet ministers and stakeholders so they would all be prepared to make decisions. Everyone was very happy that there was a deal. There was a joint cabinet meeting with the BC and Alberta governments in Alberta, which was and is a rare event, especially when the joint cabinet meeting is to celebrate a major accomplishment on which both provinces agree. At lunch-time, Coleman was walking past a meeting room when Alberta Premier Ralph Klein saw him and called him into the room.

It was a good discussion. Coleman said, "Klein says to me, 'Tell me about this softwood thing.' So I told him they were with us,

---

123 *Lumber bureau hails softwood deal; No quota on east coast exports seen as market-stabilizing move*, Campbell Morrison, *The Times-Transcript*, Moncton, NB, April 29, 2006.

4

and picking Option A, and he questioned me and I answered all his questions. Campbell and Klein have different styles in front of the media. Campbell likes to answer every question; Klein likes to hand things off to his minister. So later that day, we were in the press conference, and Campbell had been answering all the questions on the deal. Then they ask a question about softwood, so Gord starts to go to the microphone, and Ralph stops him and says, 'Gordon, you don't have to go there. We have the expert here; Rich negotiated the whole deal.' So I went to the microphone and answered the softwood questions. I didn't see Gord's face but I was told he didn't look happy."

The Alberta media, often critical of resource deals, was generally receptive to the deal even in the face of some critical comments.

> I'd have more time for the argument that Canada got hosed by the Americans in the new softwood lumber deal, announced Thursday, if we were lumber free-traders ourselves. But we're not.

> Whether or not we will admit it to ourselves, most provincial governments subsidize their logging companies by frequently selling them trees below cost.

> Most provinces, too, subsidize their lumber mills by restricting the number of raw logs that can be shipped south of the line, which both keeps the wholesale cost of logs low (by reducing the number of buyers competing for timber) and forces an artificially high number of logs to be sawed here, making our mills more profitable.

> Both of these are indirect subsidies designed to keep lumber industry jobs in Canada. That may be a noble goal, but it hardly makes us the Boy Scouts of tree trading.

There is too much glass in our trade house for us to be throwing many stones...

So Thursday's deal is likely the best one Canada could have wrung from the Americans. It doesn't conform to the spirit of the North American Free Trade Agreement (NAFTA). But neither the Americans nor we were truly seeking a deal that did.[124]

After the deal was done, Coleman acknowledged that some of the larger companies would still grumble about the fact that it was not completely free trade. "I had to sit in on the board meetings at Canfor, sit down with Jimmy Pattison and explain the deal."

He would hear them out, but he had no interest in opening up the deal because he believed it was as good as it could be, given all the factors.

As for the duties paid, "Our industry got back 80% of the duties, which was almost $5 billion. They were paid back to the companies that had paid it in. Some wanted to keep fighting over the last 20%, but I said how long do you think that would take? So we made some side agreements on research for that 20% and agreed to the 80% payout."

I did not remember that news headline: $5 billion, paid back to Canadian companies from the United States. In less than a year, he had a ten-year agreement on softwood lumber.

"My mandate in forestry was basically done, and I could turn my attention to housing."

---

124 *Softwood deal the best available*, Lorne Gunter, *Edmonton Journal*, Edmonton, AB, April 30, 2006.

Chapter 21
THE DOWNTOWN EASTSIDE

*It is critical, if we are to provide affordable housing to
our citizens, that we adapt and change our directions. It
is possible to do more for less and provide more efficient
service and more housing for our citizens. You may choose
to work with us or against us on these issues. Be aware,
however, that questions asked and information requested
and suggestions given are done so in order to provide the
best results for all of British Columbia ... If innovative land
uses and housing initiatives were to be pursued, housing
from government could actually be a net producer and not a
negative producer to the services and the provincial budget. I
have seen the good and the bad in housing delivery. I have
seen the positive impact that caring, well-managed housing
can have on people's lives.*

—Rich Coleman, First Speech in
the BC Legislature, July 6, 1996

Since the early days of settlement in the City of Vancouver, the
Downtown Eastside has had its struggles with populations with

addiction issues.[125] The unhoused population started to grow faster in the late 1990s, and by the time Coleman became the minister responsible for housing, Vancouver's Downtown Eastside was the gathering place for a confluence of marginalized people: people with substance use disorders, people with serious mental health issues, unhoused people, and urban Indigenous people. The issues were multifaceted and it would take a direct approach to try to untangle them. Coleman took a direct approach.

"I walked Vancouver's Downtown Eastside regularly, about once a month, to talk to the folks down there. I saw quite a change during my tenure, and I think that some of the strategic investments we made for the most vulnerable citizens [were] working. There's no question that we [the government of BC] were the biggest landlord in Vancouver for this kind of housing."

He initiated a program for Single-Room Occupancy (called SROs) and at that time, it was considered quite effective as an interim response.

"We did 14 new buildings on land that the City of Vancouver [had] given us, and we purchased over 20 more and renovated them, bringing them up to better standards for the residents, who are part of the most vulnerable in the city."

At the end of 2006, the Newsmaker of the Year, as named by the *Vancouver Courier*, was Homelessness. In the accompanying story, there was commentary about the planned SRO program. Interesting to note that at the time of writing of this book, the lawyer for the Pivot Legal Society, David Eby, is the premier of the province and leader of the NDP.

In April, the provincial government surprised and shocked many in the city when it announced it [had] purchased 10

---

125 *An Overview of Vancouver's Downtown Eastside for UBC Learning Exchange Trek Program Participants*, Jodi Newnham, *UBC Learning Exchange*, January 2005.

single-room occupancy hotels in the Downtown Eastside for social housing. The government made the announcement on the heels of a controversial multi-agency report, which included three provincial ministries, on the deplorable conditions of 54 hotels in the Downtown Eastside.

The Vancouver Agreement Housing Analysis Project report tallied 11,269 emergency calls in 2005 from the hotels. The report indicated welfare scams, fire code violations, and bedbug and rodent infestations.

Rich Coleman, the minister responsible for housing, promised the non-profit agencies selected to operate the provincially owned hotels would ensure they would be safe and healthy places to live.

In May, Coleman's former cabinet colleague Geoff Plant began his job as civil city commissioner. The former attorney general set his first priority as housing, outlining later in a report to council the importance of finding supportive housing for homeless people with mental health and addictions issues. "The number of homeless is growing and those with mental health and addiction problems are becoming increasingly sicker and more marginalized from the health care system," Plant said.

Outside of city hall, the issue of homelessness ignited protests from the Anti-Poverty Committee and pressure from the Pivot Legal Society to have the city protect housing stock. "Why are we paying taxes so that the city can do inspections, if they have no legal duty to inspect buildings or make sure buildings comply with city bylaws?" asked Pivot lawyer David Eby. "It's time for the city to recognize if they don't enforce the bylaws to ensure quality housing and keep rental housing open, nobody will."[126]

The City of Vancouver conducts regular inspections, and all buildings need to comply with the provincial fire code and city bylaws, fire or otherwise. Eby's comment is confusing because a quick query by his office would have revealed that the buildings require regular inspections for safety and liability purposes, including compliance with business licenses, insurance, and other paperwork. If they fail inspection, they are shut down or government is liable and can be sued for negligence. This is exactly what happened in this situation in 2023 when a restaurant was destroyed by fire, 70 people were rendered homeless, and two people died. The residents filed a class-action lawsuit and the restaurant is suing for damages and the cost of rebuilding.

The *Vancouver Sun* coverage of the BC Liberals' housing plans was more optimistic.

> There is still a long way to go, but Vancouver's seemingly insoluble homelessness problem is now one small step—or even one giant leap—closer to being solved.
>
> The provincial government announced Tuesday that, as part of an $80-million initiative to preserve and increase affordable housing, it has agreed to purchase 10 single-room occupancy hotels in Vancouver with a total of 595 rooms.
>
> The deals were struck during secret negotiations with hotel owners over the last 60 days. Some units will require renovations, at an additional estimated cost of between $5,000 and $15,000 per unit.

---

126 *Newsmaker of the Year Homelessness: [Final Edition]*, Mike Howell, *Vancouver Courier*, Vancouver, BC, December 21, 2007.

In addition, Premier Gordon Campbell said the province will purchase one SRO hotel in Victoria, four other housing units in Vancouver and Burnaby, and fund 287 planned social-housing units in Vancouver, which means Victoria will purchase or fund a total of 996 units.

Just how momentous this development is becomes clear when it's compared to the city of Vancouver's commitment to acquire one SRO hotel a year. The provincial government's announcement means that, as Mayor Sam Sullivan put it, "In one day, we've done 10 years' worth of effort."

This also means that the many people who were at risk of being evicted from SRO hotels will now be able to stay put, even during renovations.

However, despite all this good news, there is more that needs to be done. The governments must, for example, not merely commit to housing the homeless. If we don't address the factors—such as mental illness and addictions—that lead to people losing their homes, then housing becomes warehousing, with residents condemned to live out their lives in social housing, and the city and province condemned to pay for it.

With proper supports, on the other hand, many people who currently need help could well achieve self-sufficiency. Fortunately, the province seems aware of this.

Rich Coleman, the provincial minister responsible for housing, said the goal is to provide the necessary supports, including health care and addiction services, so that people "can move on to other housing types." To this end, the province plans to involve non-profit groups with experience in the operation of such hotels.[127]

About once a week for at least 12 years, sometimes in the daytime, sometimes in the evening, sometimes in the wee hours of the night, Coleman walked the Downtown Eastside. He went to the shelters and learned that they were empty in the morning and that people would show up in the evening. The system was not working for the people, because they had nowhere to go during the day, so Coleman changed the system so they were no longer closing at 7:00 a.m. and reopening at 7:00 p.m. He found operating money to keep them open during the day.

"These people are hungry. I worked to put a meal into the shelters [and] get outreach workers and have them approach people in the shelters, find out what they need. We stopped taking people who had nowhere to go and kicking them out on the street. The change was a bit of humanity. You're not cattle being put out in the field every morning."

During this time, he met a fellow that he will call John. Coleman says he was pretty bright but clearly had some issues that helped put him out on the street. Coleman tells this story, still smiling after so many years. "John had a cart. There was gravel on the sidewalk and his wheels got stuck, so I grabbed the side of the cart and helped him. We started talking and he said, 'I'm not homeless.'"

Coleman got to know John and found that he had a bit of pride, lived in an SRO, collected bottles, and had some government assistance. For a couple of years, Coleman would bump into John regularly.

"We judge them the wrong way. Sometimes it's a matter of literacy to help them get a job. The funniest story was the second or third time I bumped into John. I asked him, 'Where are you going for dinner tonight?' He said he hadn't decided. I might have

127 *B.C. government takes a big step toward making homelessness history: [Final Edition 1], The Vancouver Sun,* Vancouver, BC, April 5, 2007.

this a bit wrong, but he said something like the Salvation Army has chicken, the Gospel Mission has roast beef, and the Catholics have meat loaf. 'Which one will you go to?' I hadn't had meat loaf in a long time, so I jokingly said to him, 'How long do you have to stand in line?' He replied, 'Sometimes 45 minutes to an hour, but if the line-up is long and it's raining outside, they bring you a coffee. It's a pretty good deal!' Then he started laughing and said, 'People like you go to a restaurant and they put you at the bar and sell you some drinks and charge you some money for the drinks while you wait. Then they take you to a table and you have to wait even longer to eat and when you're done, they bring you a big bill. Sometimes you gotta wonder who the stupid people are.'

"Everyone thought the Downtown Eastside was the most unsafe place in the world. It's actually an eclectic little community. If you go to the Union Gospel Mission at Thanksgiving, you will see quite a few people, many elderly people, some from the Chinese community in Chinatown. You do have the underbelly of society, the drug dealers and dangerous people, and there are plenty of people with mental health problems. Lots of drug use. There are also a lot of nightclubs in that area that people go to.

"I never felt unsafe. I'm a big guy just walking around and talking to people. I wanted to see who the clientele were first hand, really get to know the residents and make up my own mind about what was needed to help."[128]

Keith Baldrey said Coleman's best ministerial outcome was in the housing portfolio. Given the long list of accomplishments Coleman has, this is significant. "Rich made a lot of progress [that] he didn't get credit for on the social housing file. He did make a dent in that issue, which was obscured by the controversies that were going on. It wasn't a direct portfolio; it was an add-on. Coleman was able to accomplish some things."[129]

128 Interview with Rich Coleman, February 29, 2024, in person.
129 Interview with Keith Baldrey, December 7, 2023, by Zoom.

When Coleman was in opposition, he wrote a memo on housing and sent it to the ministry. Ten years later, he was the minister responsible for housing, and he was presented with a copy of this memo by associate deputy minister Lori Wanamaker in his first meeting with her and Shane Ramsey, president and CEO of BC Housing. He remembers that she asked him if he thought the memo was still relevant, and that he replied, "Yes, and we are going to do it."

The basics of the program were about enabling people to choose where they were going to live by providing rent assistance. At the time that Coleman introduced the program, he saw that people who were waiting for affordable rentals had a long wait, so he focused on a rent assistance program where anyone making $36,000 or less per family could apply for help.

"This program didn't stigmatize people. They [were] just living in the community in regular housing. The number of homeless dropped by 6,000 people in five years and by 2016 there were 20,000 families receiving a cheque every month to assist with their rent. There were also 18,000 seniors receiving rent assistance from the province. To try to build 20,000 units in housing takes time, but allowing people to choose where to live and helping them with their rent is a lot quicker, which is a better outcome for the children."

According to Coleman, "The BC Liberal government did more for people on the social side than any other government in history. I sat in rooms with other ministers responsible for housing across Canada who said that BC had the most successful housing strategy in the country. It worked very well."

During his mandate, Coleman also set up over 1,400 units in small centres throughout BC for seniors.

"We shifted the dollars into housing for people with mental illness and concentrated the capital money into facilities that can help people with addiction or mental illness issues. We created a rent assistance program for people in shelters. There are folks who do not function well with renting in the marketplace and they need the support of a building with furniture and meals, and the help to stabilize them and help them turn their lives around. These are the most vulnerable.

"We were not a government that was about cutting ribbons. We were a government about helping people. I would never allow my ministry to take political advantage of society's most vulnerable."

A key component of Coleman's approach to housing was to connect the community, non-profits, and volunteers with the people who needed help. He developed a program that went beyond housing to add additional opportunity for jobs or net-working, and this meant bringing in outreach workers.

"When I was minister, I had outreach workers in 40 communities through BC who were focused on homeless people. When I took over, I asked if outreach workers were going into the shelters. You fish where the fish are. At that time shelters would close at 7:00 p.m. and open at 7:00 a.m. We made them 24 hours. Next it was about nutrition. I asked that we give out snacks during the day, which would bring people in and give the outreach workers a better chance to speak with them and learn what their individual needs [were]."

In addition to this holistic approach to helping people as individuals rather than as statistics, Coleman knew that when a new project was being introduced, it could be challenging to have community support for rezoning for social housing.

"Here in Langley, we did a project with buy-in, and it became a community success story. Before I was elected, I did a bunch of these things. You do a public hearing, you get a big turnout, and no one wants to say they hate poor people so they say crime, traffic problems, and public safety. So I would attend the public hearings and run them for the proponent and I would show up with all the statistics and have the answers ready. For example, if they said traffic, I would have a traffic study done and an expert to speak to it. We would get the zoning, not every time but most of the time. I ran it as a campaign when I did them."

Coleman took this experience to his job for government. "I made sure to be available as minister to anyone who needed support in social housing.

"I think it's become tougher and is different today because there are so many mental health issues. Until society does something to help people with serious issues, we are not going to be successful. I think the NDP have made it more difficult for BC Housing to get deals done. They are throwing money at them and building housing, but it's all warehousing."

During Coleman's tenure as minister responsible for housing, there was a big issue in the capital city of Victoria that escalated over a period of months. Vaughn Palmer remembers, "He dealt with a big housing encampment in Victoria. It had a chance of being a disaster because of its location. It became so nasty the TV networks would not let the cameras in because it was too dangerous."

The high-profile situation there was a political landmine. "Some activists wanted it to blow up, create a confrontation, make a story that the government was heavy-handed with these unfortunate people." [130]

The situation was a big test of Coleman's management style. As Keith Baldrey summed up, "Coleman took care of the homeless encampment. He outwaited them. He was very patient." [131]

Palmer said, "That site is a very nice playground now, a memorial for Canadians who served in Afghanistan. He got us to that point by remaining cool in the face of provocation. The government would have backed him [in] taking a tough stand. He maintained his cool, and in trying to solve the problem rather than politicizing it, he accomplished something rare." [132]

---

130 Interview with Vaughn Palmer, December 6, 2023, by Zoom.
131 Interview with Keith Baldrey, December 7, 2023, by Zoom.
132 Interview with Vaughn Palmer, December 6, 2023, by Zoom.

Luella Barnetson was a key staff member in Victoria for Coleman. She explained that the tent city issue encapsulated the issues they were managing.

"We were hearing from many people—residents, local politicians, people in other provinces—to shut down [the] tent city. But Rich was firm in his resolve. He didn't want people kicked out and left with no place to go. He wanted wraparound supports put in place for them. He wanted BC Housing staff to speak to each person and find out their story and what they needed. This was when I saw how compassionate he was, how patient he was, how understanding and kind."

It was a huge issue that dragged on over time, and Coleman had to answer publicly for the delay in resolving it, and the escalation of the problem. "There was a lot of pressure to shut down the encampment, clean up, and get things back to normal. But he understood the people living in the tents because he had talked to people living on the streets."

One dynamic that bothered Coleman was the arrival of people from other provinces who showed up to join the protest, or people who sat in the encampment to "support" the cause but actually had a home to go to at the end of the day. The supports and help that he was setting up—intended for citizens of BC who were actually without homes—were being diluted by people like this. "Their voices could not be heard. The help wasn't getting to them because of the protestors who were not really doing anything to help the people who really needed it. They were actually causing a distraction. So Rich waited, as it takes time to get through the noise, and he made sure that the people who really needed and wanted a place (as some people don't like the constrains of a place) were able to have a safe place with wraparound supports."[133]

Keivan Hirji worked closely with Coleman from November of

2015 until 2018 as ministerial advisor to the minister of natural gas development, minister responsible for housing, and deputy premier. He had a close view of many issues and remembers one day that really represented how Coleman managed to navigate politics. Coleman was co-hosting a federal and provincial government conference with Jean-Yves Duclos, the new housing minister for the federal Liberal government at the Hotel Grand Pacific in Victoria. The two governments were not getting along well at this point.

The illegal encampment on the courthouse property was quite high-profile and had been there for several months, and the individuals who were still there were protesting the government and not prepared to move. Before the meeting, Duclos's office was informed that the courthouse campsite was a sensitive issue that the province was trying to resolve, and it would be best if he didn't speak about it in the news as it could further inflame the issue and the work BC Housing was doing to resolve the issue.

> Federal Housing Minister Jean-Yves Duclos dropped by the rally, shook hands and held a "Social Housing Now" banner before being confronted about what the government planned for social housing.
>
> "We want to know how much money the Liberals are going to contribute to new social housing starts," said Vancouver housing activist Ivan Drury, who led the rally.
>
> Duclos said: "We're investing $2.3 billion over the next two years to support the housing needs of our citizens across Canada. We're working across the housing spectrum, which goes from homelessness to market housing."
>
> As he left the rally, protesters chanted: "Trudeau lies, people die."

About 40 protesters walked over to the hotel and tried to get inside and speak to the ministers. They were stopped by security and police officers who had bicycles blocking the entrance to the hotel. There was some pushing, but no one was hurt or arrested.

Later in the day, B.C. Housing Minister Rich Coleman held a news conference to conclude his meetings with the ministers and addressed the issues at tent city.

"My wish is we get some form of direction from the courts so we can complete a process over the next week or 10 days so people can move into homes," he said.[134]

After Duclos left the demonstration and made his way back into the hotel, tensions escalated. The protesters were galvanized and at the front door yelling. Meanwhile, people were trying to get into the hotel and were being pushed around by the protesters. The hotel went into lockdown.

Jean-Yves Duclos and Rich were in different rooms in the hotel. Shane Ramsey of BC Housing and Evan Siddal of CMHC were in the building for the meetings.

Keivan Hirji remembers Coleman asking him to step in. "Rich said, 'Go ask Evan what the hell his minister was doing out there. This table is here to build a relationship between two levels of government and he's outside making things worse for us.'[135]

"Somehow cooler heads came together. Everyone acknowledged it was a catastrophic public relations disaster. The hotel was on lockdown and we could have just ended the discussion.

---

134 *Tent city fate caught in legal limbo; Judge reserves judgment on bid to close camp; province offers more housing units,* Sarah Petrescu, *Times-Colonist,* Victoria, BC, June 29, 2016.

135 Interview with Keivan Hirji, April 21, 2021.

Rich had a lot of influence in the room and among other housing ministers from across the country at that point and could have taken complete control of the agenda, and instead he pushed aside the tension. BC was already seen as a leader because a lot of the models we were using in BC, the feds wanted to adopt [those] across the country. It ended up going quite well. We managed to negotiate a useful dynamic between the provinces and the federal government that was in the best interests of housing."[136]

By 2024, the homeless and unfit housing crisis in Vancouver had escalated, and many of the SRO programs were targeted as part of the problem. David Eby, as premier, announced plans to phase them out and replace them with "dignified housing." At the time of writing, the government is at the review stage. There is no definition of what dignified housing is, nor is there a timeframe to implement the changes that they have not yet articulated.

> The B.C. government has committed to undertaking a review into how single-room-occupancy hotels or SROs are operated in the province.
>
> An estimated 7,000 people live in Vancouver's SROs in 156 buildings.
>
> Many of the buildings are aging and in desperate need of repair and maintenance, and housing officials are calling for better oversight and management.
>
> When asked about the issue on Monday, Premier David Eby said SROs are not "fit housing."

---

136 Interview with Keivan Hirji, April 22, 2021, by phone with email follow-up.

"We need to have a plan for phasing out these SROs and replacing them with dignified housing and that's exactly what we're doing," Eby said.

Eby said the lengthy process is not acceptable to British Columbians but it is going to take some time to make real change. [137]

By Eby's own admission, the Downtown Eastside has never been worse.[138]

Coleman's work in housing was generally recognized as significant in building models between the public and private sector and including non-profits. There were controversies and much more work to do after he set the foundation; however, he helped thousands of people, including families and seniors, by putting in place a new policy.

Keivan Hirji was only days into his job as ministerial assistant when he was handed Coleman's constituency files. Every MLA approaches constituency work differently; some use these files for local profile, always focused on re-election by connecting each problem into a possible "win" and announcing progress in order to build support before the next election.

Hirji remembers going through the first files with Coleman. "He gave straightforward direction and said, 'Let's help these people out.' He said to me, 'I never want to politicize these files,' referring to the housing files. That was his strongest message: Keep politics out of it."

Coleman's commitment to helping people on an individual level extended beyond his own constituency. Hirji soon learned

---

137 'Replace with dignified housing': Vancouver's SROs need to be phased out, says B.C.'s premier, Christa Dao and Amy Judd, *Global News*, January 10, 2023.

138 'Haven't seen it worse': BC premier promises help is coming for the Downtown Eastside, Claire Fenton, *Daily Hive*, January 11, 2023. https://dailyhive.com/vancouver/downtown-eastside-sro-phased-out

that what mattered was solving the real problems, one by one, and that Coleman saw this as part of his job as an MLA. "He never asked me when I brought a file forward to him which MLA was responsible. He once had a conversation with [NDP MLA] Selina Robinson about a housing file while in the house. When he got back to the office, he asked me to head over to MLA Robinson's office asap to get more information and figure out how to help. It really didn't matter to him where the constituency file came from, whether our caucus or opposition. It was just about the file.

"He was really clear about how we approach the ministry work as well. He told me, 'We don't politicize the housing file whatsoever. Housing is too important.'"

When asked about the results obtained in the housing portfolio while he held it, whether at the provincial, local, or individual level, Coleman focuses on the staff. "I was able as minister to put together new housing because I had such a great team. You have to let your people do their job and you have to let them know you will let them. It's amazing what people will do when they are empowered to do it."

"I've always believed that."

Chapter 22
2011 AND THE 2013 ELECTION

Wise leaders generally have wise counselors because it takes
a wise person themselves to distinguish them.

—Diogenes of Sinope, Cynic Philosopher,
around 350BC

In 2016 I released my third book on BC politics called *Christy Clark: Behind the Smile.* In that book, I spent a lot of time on the 2011 leadership race and the surprise win in the 2013 election of the BC Liberals under Christy Clark's leadership. Because there are so many topics in *That's Rich* that have not been covered elsewhere, I am deliberately limiting the information in this chapter to new information specific to Rich Coleman's role in the BC Liberal leadership race in 2011 and his interaction with the 2013 general election as campaign co-chair.

On November 3, 2010, BC Liberal Leader Gordon Campbell announced that he was resigning from his position as party leader as soon as the party could elect a new leader. His announcement was a surprise, and it came in the wake of polls showing that his popularity had dropped dramatically after his government introduced the HST, a harmonized sales tax that he had previously said he would not introduce.[139] He had been leader since 1993, and many praised his legacy.

Campbell's resignation came two weeks before a planned party convention, which was then cancelled. He had been such a strong leader, controlling the reigns of power from the premier's office, that there were no obvious successors when he announced his resignation. He had just shuffled his cabinet and broadcast a television address in the week before his announcement, and his government had scheduled a referendum on the HST for September of 2011. Coleman's name was on the short list of possible contenders.

> There is a cadre of experienced cabinet ministers who are mulling leadership runs. George Abbott is affable and competent. He never takes himself too seriously. Maybe it's time to start.

> Shirley Bond could take a flyer, on behalf of women and northerners.

> Rich Coleman has built an impressive power base within the party. He will definitely be a kingmaker, if not the king.

> Mike de Jong is a career pro in the attorney general's portfolio, which often produces contenders.

> Kevin Falcon looks like he's been wanting this since elementary school. Mary Polak is equally as ambitious.[140]

---

139 *Embattled B.C. premier resigns in surprise move; Politics Popularity plummeted after introduction of HST*, Lindsay Kines and Rob Shaw, *Telegraph-Journal*, Saint John, NB, November 4, 2010.

140 *Who will lead? B.C. Liberals need a fresh face*, Les Leyne, *Times-Colonist*, Victoria, BC, November 4, 2010.

Vaughn Palmer noted, "He thought of running for leader himself and then he didn't run. It is interesting to try to understand why he didn't run."

Coleman said there were many factors that led to him deciding not to run and to support Falcon instead.

"After Campbell resigned I was thinking of running. I had funders, I had an airplane, and I had support. My biggest fear was that I saw how much of a toll it took on families. I saw how wound-up Michele would get if there was a negative news story, and realized how much more of an issue it would be if I became premier. Then I heard from different sources that Campbell was quietly pushing Falcon. That was a significant disappointment for me. I think the least he could have done was leave the field open. Then, a couple of my colleagues let me down."

Coleman is known for his loyalty and his skills in fundraising and organizing. He had expected that, given how much he had delivered to others, they would step up to support him if he decided to run. He had, in fact, funded a whole bunch of election campaigns that were successful in electing MLAs. Many of the candidates and their organizations did not know how to raise enough money, so he would take the financial pressure off by filling their coffers.

Coleman was blunt in stating the facts on this. "I was very successful at raising money. Since 1996, I took care of making sure we provided seed funds for a series of ridings. In one election, 30 ridings were supported out of Fort Langley–Aldergrove. Over my time in office, over 40 ridings were funded out of my riding and team. Even the small ridings, when we knew they would not win, we would send them $5,000 so they could have the basics for the campaign."

He was the definition of a team player, and he also knew that a winning campaign needed money. He was always focused on the win for the team.

Fundraising was foundational to Coleman's political organization. He was motivated to set it up as part of his political strategy because he was owed money after the 1996 election when he secured little bits of campaign debt—not enough money had been raised. "After 1996, I was personally owed $12,000 in a line of credit where I had assembled little bits of debt. I had a meeting at a restaurant and people were telling me Campbell had to go, he [couldn't] get it done. I said no, we need to think of it as a business, with ridings around us needing help getting organized. We need to help them by teaching them how to fundraise and set up basic organization. So that's where it started and it continued from there."

When Campbell resigned, the same colleagues who had benefited from Coleman's support let him down. "I was frustrated. Mary Pollak called me up and [said] she [was] supporting Falcon. That was frustrating because she wasn't from Langley. I got her the nomination, I put her team together because Campbell wanted her in. She didn't have money so I transferred $40K in to make sure she was funded.

"Shirley Bond [was] the next disappointment. When she arrived in Victoria, we took care of her—me, Bill Barrisoff, and Rich Thorpe. She was elected on a wave, [then] she [had] to build an organization with no money. I was with my team at a convention in Whistler. We invited her to a meeting and told her we were going to get her funded and organized.

"Michele was pretty upset and called Bond to tell her how bad it was she didn't support."

Coleman was well connected in the federal Conservative party. The last consideration for him was when Senator Gerry St. Germain, who was a good friend, invited him for coffee with Kevin Falcon and one other Conservative.

"During the meeting, they said they only wanted one of us to run because they did not want to split the Conservative vote. They suggested the younger one should run. I was overweight and had just learned I had Type 2 diabetes. Did I want it bad enough? Kevin and I had coffee and I said if you really want it, I will step back. I think for my family it was the best thing. I could see that running for leader would have added a lot of stress to Michele.

"At the same time, it was really disappointing."

While Les Leyne's article listing potential replacements had a headline saying the BC Liberals needed a fresh face, Christy Clark's name was not on the list of possible outsiders. Rumours of dissent within caucus could not be proven, and the party quickly moved on to its plans for the leadership race and convention. The date for the vote was set for February 26, less than four months after Campbell's announcement, and the party executive had also decided to call an extraordinary convention to modernize the constitution. The leadership vote would have a weighted voting system.[141]

Rich Coleman backed Kevin Falcon for leader of the Liberals, and when Christy Clark won, there was a lot of speculation that the coalition of Conservatives and Liberals would fall apart. Clark put together a cabinet after her victory that included Falcon in the positions of deputy premier and minister of finance, while Rich Coleman kept energy and mines, plus housing.[142] Her cabinet reflected the ongoing coalition, and the big problems started in the run-up to the 2013 election, when many of the BC Liberal MLAs announced they would not seek re-election. When Coleman stayed loyal, many were surprised. He took on the position of co-chair of the election campaign, working alongside high-profile federal Liberal campaigner Mark Marissen.

Coleman stepped up with strong support of Christy Clark. As Palmer said in an understated manner, "Christy Clark leaned on him a lot. It was controversial that he supported her."

---

141 *BC Liberals pick new leader Feb. 26*, anonymous, *Terrace Standard*, Terrace, BC, November 16, 2010.

142 *Clark puts together a reasonable first cabinet*, Paul Willcocks, *Alaska Highway News*, Fort St. John, BC, March 18, 2011.

Coleman vividly recalls the news conference when he announced his plans to stay. "In 2012, I remember looking around at the faces of the media in the scrum and seeing how disappointed they were that I was staying. When I said, 'And we are going to win,' they were scornful.

"There were people very disappointed that I stayed. It took a while for some of them to come back on board. It was tough times for a while.

"You don't trash your organization and something you believe in just because someone doesn't like someone. If you join an organization to support its beliefs, you need to stay for the sake of the organization. Your ego should not get in the way."

An important part of Coleman's support for Clark was his network. He unleashed his fundraising and organizational skills to support her and the BC Liberals' re-election. It paid off with the BC Liberals' surprise win of a majority government. Coleman did very well in his riding, winning a fifth term.

Rich Coleman felt vindicated when the results started pouring for the provincial election.

The incumbent for Fort Langley–Aldergrove said B.C. voters agreed with him that the Liberals and leader Christy Clark were the best choices for B.C.

"It shows the people actually see the leadership of Christy Clark, my leader, but they also see just how strong our message was," Coleman said.

He said Clark did a "marvelous job as a campaigner for us" and "she's just a great leader."

In his fifth election, Coleman hung onto his seat handily. On Tuesday night, Elections BC results showed Coleman with 14,533 while the next nearest finish was NDP candidate Shane Dyson with 6,700.[143]

Coleman had worked hard to keep the focus on retaining government after the change in leadership. "The biggest adjustment with her leadership was the difficult time she had to spend with a group of people who were very disloyal. These were people who wanted to re-fight the leadership race. They just needed to move on, so we could get on with governing. My role was to be one of the people who [kept] it all together. Those of us who could see the bigger picture stayed with her, but there were others who were really disloyal and their behaviour reflected that."

After the 2013 election, Christy Clark placed Coleman in such a strong position that the Vancouver Sun wrote a feature story on him, calling him minister of everything.

> Even his brother doubted him. But when the polls came in on May 14 it was clear that Rich Coleman had been right all along – the B.C. Liberals were returning to power with a renewed mandate. The imposing Fort Langley-Aldergrove MLA will be a cornerstone of Premier Christy Clark's government – deputy premier, minister for natural gas development, minister responsible for housing, and a member of four senior cabinet committees.

One of Coleman's strongest qualities is his support for women as equal players in politics. Many may assume that this quality is common; however, women in politics know that it is not.

---

143 *Coleman celebrates fifth victory; The MLA for Fort Langley-Aldergrove returns to Victoria to represent this riding,* Heather Colpitts, *Langley Advance,* Langley, BC, May 16, 2013.

Sheila Orr admired Coleman's attitude. Orr was a candidate for the BC Liberals in 1996 and was elected MLA from 2001 to 2005, losing a re-election bid to Rob Fleming in 2005. "He is a huge supporter of women running in politics. Not only morally, [but] he was a big financial supporter to me. He really helped me out. He didn't just pay lip service to women running in politics—he really believed it and acted on it.

"This is a big man who is an ex-cop, and the first thing you think is that he is tough. The perception of Rich Coleman is totally the opposite to the reality of Rich Coleman.

"When I was in government, I set up PEERS [Prostitutes Empowerment Education and Resource Society] and I said to Gordon Campbell that I would like caucus to meet some of these sex trade workers, bring them in to the caucus meeting. So I brought them in for a meeting and maybe nine people showed up. Gordon Campbell and Rich Coleman were both there. When you sit with sex trade workers you have to understand they are just people, and they have a story. These women shared their stories.

"Rich was engaged and was supportive of these hardcore issues. He really listened to them."[144]

Christy Clark respected and admired Coleman for his loyalty and consistency. She was taken aback by him at first because of how he came across in the early years of the BC Liberals, when Campbell was leader. "I was bowled over by his bluster and his loudness and I never really got to know him. Like we weren't natural buddies really, because at the time you were you Liberal or Conservative. He was a hardcore Conservative and I was an active federal Liberal and so we were in different bubbles."[145]

Later, Clark learned there were more layers to Coleman, and she relied on him in many ways to take on the toughest portfolios and trust him with some of the biggest challenges.

144 Interview with Sheila Orr, April 22, 2021, by phone.
145 Interview with Christy Clark, May 29, 2021, by Zoom.

"Rich had such strong skills at wrangling people. He is a master strategist at getting things done, figuring out how to get everyone working on the team. That quality was absolutely vital for government."

Coleman was always connected to bringing in money, whether through fundraising for a community, the political party, or attracting money to British Columbia in the private sector. Clark noted, "The investor community really liked him. He's so approachable. He has that big presence. The investment community overseas took to him immediately. Whether in Asia or Europe, they all liked him."

Clark trusted Coleman completely for his loyalty and said there was not a moment when she worried he would undermine her.

Orr noted that Coleman put people before politics. "Rich Coleman is also a Conservative and I'm not. He was always respectful of that and helped me out even when he must have disagreed with me on some of these issues. He would back me up. He had more influence than I did, so I used it and he let me.

"When I sat on [the] Treasury Board, he would support me on what I brought forward, like raising monthly allowances. I don't remember them all, but he would support me on issues that were basically left-leaning. He knew they mattered to people.

"That's the reality of Rich Coleman."

Chapter 23
LNG

Leadership is the capacity to translate vision into reality.

—Warren Bennis

There were many critics of the BC Liberals' plans to put Liquified Natural Gas (LNG) projects in BC. Coleman took this as a challenge, and his attitude from the beginning was, "I'm going to prove you all wrong. We are going to get it done." And he did. It was a long road, though, with many more challenges than expected. Coleman took the lead on behalf of the province. He attributes the vision to Christy Clark, and she attributes the heavy lifting to him.

Vaughn Palmer commented. "Coleman was an important player when it came to LNG. Christy Clark had made a huge promise to deliver significantly with respect to developing an LNG industry.

"They set high expectations, then they had a tough time. We had a long struggle to even get the first project, and Coleman managed to get the first project started. Coleman carried the file with a lot of enthusiasm. [He] had good feedback and lots of expressions of interest."

There were many layers of regulatory problems at all levels of government and across ministries. There was also the First Nations issue of land, environmental, economic, and social jurisdiction.

Palmer saw these as key to the rollout. "When it came to executing on this interest, the regulatory and Indigenous obstacles were so huge that we missed the main window of opportunity. You can see that by the places where LNG was established. This part is not Coleman's fault because it was outside of his control, but it had a huge impact on his effectiveness."[146]

Palmer noted that BC and Louisiana were both pursuing LNG around the same time, 2011, and since Louisiana had terminals to retrofit for exporting, they started exporting in 2016, while BC's Kitimat terminal is scheduled to start in 2025. Meanwhile, the pipeline is not done yet.

Coleman's imagination was captured by Clark's vision on LNG from the time she began talking about it in 2011. They spent time exploring its viability in the two years before the election, and as they reached outside BC, he remembered that it took some time to gain the interest of people in the international community, which was necessary to have a chance to build an entire plan. It takes leadership.

"It's gutsy, because LNG is not going to happen in an election cycle, so you can't get an easy 'political win.' These multi-billion-dollar decisions don't happen overnight. It was Clark's initial vision that said we are going to make this happen."

Coleman was passionate about doing his part to realize the massive opportunity that LNG represented to BC, given the reserves contained within our region. He saw it as a win for BC and a win for the world.

"You have a resource that you can sell, a massive resource, and you have countries around the world that are quite literally choking on smoke from their energy sources. The right thing to do is to work for the people you represent; improve the GDP and the job situation; finance your healthcare and education; and

---

146 Interview with Vaughn Palmer, December 6, 2023, by Zoom.

supply the energy to the countries that need it. Long-term vision-wise, it is the right thing to do. This is about the next generation of British Columbians and the generation after that. This is going to provide for my children and my children's children.

"This is going to be one of the most dramatic shifts in economic development in my lifetime."

Christy Clark knew she was setting up a huge workload for Coleman, and she recognized the lack of infrastructure. "Rich was capable of doing a big job. LNG was the biggest job in government because we were starting from scratch. If you are ministry of forestry or mining, it might have complicated regulations, but it existed. In this case, there was nothing to reference and everything to do.

"We had to build a tax regime out of nothing. We had to find investment out of nothing and build an environmental regime out of nothing.

"There were no reference points. We were starting a whole new industry. No one has done that. The only comparable thing in BC history was the dam system that W.A.C. Bennett started in the 1950s, but otherwise everything else already existed."

Clark knew she could rely on Coleman's people skills and ability to integrate systems. She put herself as chair of the LNG committee for cabinet and they met every week, with one task specifically targeted at overcoming the silos of government by meeting regularly and having constructive communication. Everyone at the table would report out on their responsibilities. If Clark could not make the meetings, she knew Coleman would be overseeing the process and make sure everyone was on track.[147]

"It takes time to work with so many different ministers and ministries. There's no way around it. You have to sit down and talk to people. There's no substitute for the hard work. He was a genius at shepherding everyone."

---

147 Interview with Christy Clark, ibid.

The difference in culture in Asia and the fact that Clark was female were sometimes parts of the meeting dynamics. There were times when Asian bankers and investors would defer to Coleman in the meeting, even if they had been briefed that the person in charge was the female member of the delegation.

"When they did defer to Rich, he would say that they had to ask his boss, the premier. He would make a point of making it clear I was in charge. He knew what to do and he didn't like it if he thought I was being disrespected because of my gender."

Coleman worked very closely with the investors to help with the viability planning. His ministry was working with the companies to understand the next step in the investment decision process. How are they going to power up? Is there an environmental impact?

Mike Morris provided some insights into Coleman's strategy in managing the big companies and projects. Enbridge is one of the biggest energy companies in the world, employing over 12,000 people in Canada, and it is heavily invested in natural gas pipeline projects in BC. Before Morris was elected, he was suing Enbridge and had been through years of court actions that were settled out of court around the same time he decided to run for office. He had outlined this in his candidate application documents, and Coleman had read through everything before Morris was approved to run for the BC Liberals.

Morris recalled the background to the lawsuit. "Prior to my retirement from the RCMP, I was going to build a lodge and cabins on five sites on three different lakes, connected by walking trails. I had gone through a lengthy process to get licenses from the government; had the geotech work to get the necessary permits for the water and wastewater systems; and had an excavator in there to do the early work. Right when I finished the geotech work, Enbridge announced the pipeline and it was going right through the middle of my lodge. I thought they had done this by mistake so I approached them to move it and they said no. They had been using my trails to mark their route."

Over the years of litigation, Morris and the key officials at Enbridge had become quite well acquainted. Coleman did not speak to Morris about this file; however, shortly after Morris was elected, Coleman was meeting with Enbridge so they could lay out their pipeline plan. The story is one among many of Coleman, the strategist.

"I was asked to come in about ten minutes into the meeting, and I had no background about the meeting. I was the MLA for Prince George—Mackenzie, he was the person responsible for natural gas. There was quite a bit of shock when I walked into the room. Rich had a chair beside him, so I sat with him. Rich didn't pause. He kept going in the meeting... They seemed hesitant to talk with me there, but the meeting went ahead. It was an opportunity to hear from Enbridge on the Northern Gateway pipeline. The reason he asked me to come was probably for effect. Here's someone who knows Enbridge intimately, and I think he thought I would be someone who could knock Enbridge off their game."[148]

In a move that surprised many, Christy Clark's government hired former Liberal leader Gordon Wilson to work on the LNG file. Wilson had re-emerged in public life during the 2013 election to call on all Liberals to "come home" to support Christy Clark. It was a video statement that caught a lot of attention, and many attributed his appointment to his re-engagement with the party after Campbell left. Christy Clark had been part of Wilson's core team before the 1991 election breakthrough, and that was part of the dynamic for his return. Wilson, a staunch Liberal, was now working under the portfolio of Coleman, a staunch Conservative who also saw Wilson as one reason for the 1996 election loss to

---

148 Interview with Mike Morris, April 22, 2021, by Zoom.

Glen Clark. He came into the position with a strong impression of Coleman and it changed over time.

The first meeting between Wilson and Coleman set the tone for the working relationship. "I had a call from the premier's office in Vancouver to go meet at the cabinet offices. When I entered the cabinet chamber, Coleman was sitting at the head of the table. I felt like I was Scrooge being escorted in to meet the Ghost of Christmas Present, since Coleman was larger than life and taking up the head of the table, with some scattered minions around him, and a couple of other cabinet ministers and a deputy minister present. This is when Coleman articulated to me what his vision of the LNG Buy BC program was going to be. Two things I remember him saying: There's no room for mavericks, and at the end of the day, the premier gets credit for whatever happens."[149]

Wilson left with a clear impression of who was in charge of the direction of the whole program. "At the time, I believed I was going to be working with the LNG taskforce. It was a few days later that I was told I would not be working with Coleman at all. I was not to have any contact with Coleman, nor was I to have any contact with any of the proponents. I was instead deployed to the ministry responsible for jobs training."[150]

Although Wilson did not work directly with Coleman, they were often at meetings together and their respective teams interacted quite a bit. Wilson was working for Shirley Bond, then minister of jobs, tourism, and skills training, as one of the bureaucrats responsible for developing capacity in the workforce and assisting with community support for the program through educational opportunity development.

"As I had a chance to observe Coleman in public meetings, and afterward in the debrief… I saw that there was a lot more to him than the caricature of the 'political fixer.' I am not sure why it

149 Interview with Gordon Wilson, May 11, 2021, in person.
150

shocked me, but it did, that he was so dedicated to his family and kids. He has a great sense of humour, which was a surprise."

Wilson also had different experiences to bring to the team, and they gave him a new perspective. "Having sat in the chair of minister and seen the civil service from that side of the desk, it was remarkably different to be sitting as a civil servant and watching the interaction of the minister with senior staff. What I learned was that not all civil servants treat their ministers with a great deal of respect. Most are professional in their work, but after hours when they talk about politicians, some of them are pretty blunt about their impressions of their ministers, and it is not positive. What surprised me was how highly regarded Coleman was by his senior civil servants, the ones who worked most closely with him. It was not because they were political or partisan. They were strictly non-partisan. It was because he treated them with respect."[151]

There was considerable private sector interaction with the BC government. Coleman, as was his habit, developed solid personal working relationships with many of the industry leaders. One was Andy Calitz, CEO of LNG Canada, which was a division of Shell. "He called me the quarterback. Sometimes you have to trust people, especially when they are worried about elements [of] a deal. He could come to me with his concerns, knowing it was in a confidential manner, and we could solve it together. I understood that Calitz was accountable to his investors."[152]

Calitz moved from LNG Canada to Royal Dutch Shell in 2019, and from Vancouver to a place south of London in the United Kingdom. He lived in BC for six years, arriving just after Christy Clark's surprise victory, and during his tenure frequently travelled to Calgary to help develop the project. He was aware of the high profile that LNG had before, during, and after the 2013 election.

Calitz met with Coleman many times on the LNG Canada

151 Interview with Gordon Wilson, May 11, 2021, in person.
152 Interview with Rich Coleman, April 2, 2021, by Zoom.

project, which was one of three major projects he oversaw for Shell. The first two were Sakhalin, Russia and Gorgon, Australia. He proceeded with caution. "In the role of international project development, I have learned not to get too close to political party people. I always ask myself, 'What happens if there is a critical change?' Must be able to work with whomever is in charge. I have learned with major projects in LNG, there are plenty of people who want to be involved in each project, but only two or three who can actually take it to FID because they have the focus and abilities."[153]

Even with Calitz's experience in Russia and the layers of challenges there, he recognized that the LNG project in Canada was complicated for some of the same reasons, including trust, culture, and language. When he first met the re-elected government, both Clark and Coleman were focused on the new mandate, with a lot of work to do in LNG, which had been a big part of the election platform. The most advanced project was Pacific Northwest (PNW) LNG, led by Petronas, a global energy player headquartered in Kuala Lumpur, Malaysia and operating in over 100 companies globally.

"We deliberately established ourselves as a strong Vancouver presence. Quite different from PNWLNG. First task? I had to trust them and they needed to trust me. Second part, I need[ed] someone in local government who [understood] the province inside out. Rich [had] seen it through housing, crime, gambling, newspaper, legislature, so many eyes through which has he [had] seen BC."

Coleman was a good resource for Calitz, who was careful to keep the relationship professional and constructive. "You have to be careful not to get too close to someone, [and] at the same time develop a level of trust where someone can advise of any potential

---

153 Interview with Andy Calitz, July 20, 2021, by Zoom.

issues. The team of Christy and Rich did this very well. Had two brilliant people on my team, Susanna Pierce and Jared Kuehl. The personal chemistry between the BC LNG team and LNG Canada was an important dynamic in the project's progress."

"Rich was very accessible… He had a table at the Fairmont Pacific where we would often have coffee and talk things through. It was near my office and his office, and we would meet often and the conversations were productive. Rich was on top of the engagements in other projects. He never inappropriately discussed other projects, [which] would have eroded my trust in him, but he kept me informed on political developments in the province as needed."

The LNG Canada team quickly understood that Coleman and Clark were strong politicians. Calitz said the first impression he had of Coleman was his deep care for the province of BC. He also believed that while Coleman had a deep understanding of British Columbia, he did not have a deep understanding of LNG. This was something that would develop over time.

"Rich and Christy's expectations of what LNG would do for the province were a mile high in an employment dimension, a First Nations dimension, capacity-building, links to Asia, enhanced taxation, a future prosperity fund."

There were many challenges in the pursuit of LNG in BC that were outside the control of any government. In 2016, oil prices crashed. At that time, LNG Canada had made some progress, but the decision was made to pause the work. Calitz had to deliver the news to Clark and Coleman before it went public, and he told them he was staying in BC through the pause.

"If I had left, the project would have stopped. I still remember the disappointment in their faces when I told them the project was paused. It was profound. They went into the 2017 election largely empty-handed in terms of an energy LNG project."[154]

---

154 Interview with Andy Calitz, ibid.

The delay was big news, and not good news for Coleman or Clark.

> The LNG Canada joint venture led by Royal Dutch Shell PLC has delayed its final investment decision on exporting liquefied natural gas from Kitimat in northern British Columbia.

> Andy Calitz, LNG Canada's chief executive officer, had been scheduled to announce a decision on whether to proceed with the project by the end of this year.

> But on Monday, he said there isn't any new target set to determine when there might be a revised timeline.[155]

Years later, Calitz has a clear recall of the specific players and their responsibilities as the foundation of BC's LNG industry was established. "The roles of the three people who helped make LNG Canada happen during the Clark era were quite diverse. Christy was the perfect host for international visitors. Rich was the anchoring man who kept things calm, was responsible for First Nations engagement, and [problem-solved] on certain files. Steve Carr carried the file to make sure it met tax, environmental, labour, regulatory, and other matters, and they all worked collaboratively with our team."[156]

Andy Calitz understood that the BC Liberals had a vision about something for the province that included additional diversification of the economy. He expressed his perception that they built a broad-based team, maintained focus, and executed their plan on all fronts in an effort to make it happen, including First

155 *Shell-backed LNG Canada delays plans for terminal on B.C. coast*, Brent Jang, *The Globe and Mail* (Online), July 11, 2016.
156 Interview with Andy Calitz, July 20, 2021, by Zoom with email follow-up.

Nations engagement; industrial training; and many trips to Asia to engage with Chinese, Korean, Japanese, and other potential investors. He believes that Coleman's role was very significant in bringing the vision to life.

"The vision was exceptional. Rich considers his comments, talks slowly, and has a good sense of where risk lies. Rich understands the art of the possible."[157]

---

157 Interview with Andy Calitz, ibid.

Chapter 24
FIRST NATIONS AND POLITICS

Together, Canadians must do more than just talk about reconciliation; we must learn how to practise reconciliation in our everyday lives—within ourselves and our families, and in our communities, governments, places of worship, schools, and workplaces. To do so constructively, Canadians must remain committed to the ongoing work of establishing and maintaining respectful relationships.

—The Truth and Reconciliation
Commission of Canada[158]

Like the BC Liberals in 2006 when they lost an election they had expected to win, after their 2013 defeat the NDP were relentless in their "search-and-destroy" attack strategy for taking on every issue the BC Liberals pursued and targeting every key player, throwing as many negative allegations as possible at them to destroy credibility and prevent momentum. The highest-profile government agenda item was LNG, and the two people most attached to its advancement were Christy Clark and Rich Coleman. It became

---

158 *Final Report of the Truth and Reconciliation Commission of Canada, Volume One,* Truth and Reconciliation Commission of Canada. Summary: "Honouring the Truth, Reconciling for the Future."

one of the three favourite targets for allegations of government corruption or negligence, the other two being money laundering in casinos and out-of-control Asian investment in the housing market for property flipping.

Woven into the LNG project development was the issue of First Nations' collaboration and economic development. It was essential to have this collaboration for any project to advance, and the BC Liberals had evolved considerably in their public policy on First Nations from their days of suing to block the Nisga'a Treaty. In fact, a primary consideration in all resource projects was Indigenous accommodation. The minister who led the outreach and relationship-building with Indigenous people was Coleman.

Christy Clark remembered, "The folks in the Indigenous community of LNG really like him. He worked well with them and listened to them."

The *Financial Post*, a national newspaper focused on business, did a feature piece on LNG, and Claudia Cattaneo, the *Financial Post*'s western business columnist, took a deep dive into the complex issues involving industry development. Coleman confirmed the government's commitment in his answers.

Q: LNG also involves lots of challenges, including relating to First Nations who are often opposed to energy development. Is this one area where you are going to let the market sort things out, or will the province play a leadership role?

A: We are going to be leaders with industry to try and get it done…We will try and help with the process as best we can and we are happy to help on the First Nations consultation and accommodation piece because the Crown has that responsibility anyway and our folks are very engaged.

Q: What can you do with First Nations?

A: The reality is that First Nations aren't that different from us. They want to see jobs and economic activity for their families. They'd like to see training... It brings us to a co-operative, workable environment versus an adversarial one.

Q: Is there a right way and a wrong way to interact with First Nations?

A: In B.C., we have to consult with First Nations and accommodate... It's a way of doing business because we don't have treaties [in many areas]. Even in the areas where we do have treaties, we still do a lot of consulting and accommodation because treaties... written 100 years ago aren't necessarily relevant to what is going on in the land today... [I]f you are respectful and if you work with First Nations, are honest and fair, you will get a deal.

Q: There is limited space on the B.C. coast where LNG developers can load large tankers and build facilities. Would you make Crown land available to promote this industry?

A: Something like 97% of the B.C. land base is Crown. And so if there needs to be land available, we have no hesitation to sitting down and negotiating... If there was an opportunity to increase jobs and economic activity and part of it was in relationship to Crown land, we would look favourably on the investment.

The relentless attacks on Coleman as he advanced the LNG file were noisy and inflammatory. Clark recalled, "Rich was defending it in the house. The NDP were attacking it every day. We were under siege about LNG. Today people don't remember that, but they were after us constantly and he was responding, in detail, every day."

Gordon Wilson had a front-row seat, and by the nature of his job, was not allowed to speak out about the file. He of course followed the political developments closely and knew the players in the NDP very well, since he had been a cabinet minister working with many of them less than 15 years previously.

Wilson said, "Initially the NDP took the position that the LNG plans were rhetoric and 'pie in the sky.' Later... when the Green Party began to voice environmental concerns, the NDP had to shift their position or lose support to the Greens.

"The NDP started to vocally oppose all LNG development. Their MLAs and MPs, especially in the north, and the leadership in the legislature, began campaigns against LNG.

"The nature of the campaign was to sow as much misinformation into the public discourse as possible, to make the industry sound so horrific that even reasonable people would have to say there must be some basis to the claims. As soon as members of the public are asking, 'How bad is it?' you have lost the conversation, because it is now associated with the word 'bad.'"

Regardless of the campaign against these efforts, the projects continued to advance—a lot of work was underway negotiating agreements with First Nations all over northern BC for LNG and other resource-based projects, including gas pipelines. Wilson's role expanded in part as a response to the growth in opposition to the projects. One of the areas that generated good public engagement was the development of sessions to put facts into the discussion. The government quickly saw the need for public "myth-busting" sessions, with public open houses where they could take the facts to the public and explain the benefits and objectives of LNG. Coleman and the LNG Task Force, plus their staff, were responsible for all new areas of engagement to put information in front of the private sector, engage with First Nations communities, and provide public sessions.

One of these sessions led to an iconic story of Coleman's engagement while travelling the province. His ministerial assistant Keivan Hirji recalls a story in the territory of the Lax Kw'alaams First Nation, who were key to the Petronas PNWLNG project near Prince Rupert.

There were two meetings scheduled, a town hall in the village and one the next evening in Prince Rupert. At these meetings, there were staff from PNW; Spencer Sproule, a gentleman from Petronas, and others connected to the project; Simon Coley, Dave Nikolejsin, and Doug Caul from Indigenous relations; and Gordon Wilson as the advocate.

We arrived in Lax Kw'alaams, a beautiful village with an amazing community, but the hardship in the community was visible. You see the canneries that have closed down; you hear the stories of job loss and other social challenges. We arrived at the rec centre, like a work base camp. We were looking for a cup of coffee. We saw a sign on a house that said "coffee" so we asked the gentleman if he sells coffee and he said, "Sure, but I have to go get the beans." When we asked how long that would take, he said about three hours. He had to go to Prince Rupert. That gave me a pretty good idea how remote the village was from everything.

I remember standing on the shoreline. Someone said, "If you look across there you might see Alaska." You could feel how cut off it was. There were only a few ferry trips that ran during the day.

There was a guy travelling with us, an LNG scientist, and we had been trying to get on this ferry run by the Village of Lax Kw'alaams. A bunch of people piled on before us in their cars. The science guy didn't make it, but we did. So we set up shop at the rec centre, and an elder walked in to talk to us. He came in wearing a plaid shirt that was unbuttoned [and] some jeans, and [he] started asking what we were doing, and about LNG. He seemed very curious and Rich answered all his questions.

Later we had the town hall and it was a disaster. The loudest people in the room monopolized the conversation. I remember one woman standing up asking about the second pipeline, and when she was asked what she meant, she said, 'What about the one you are planning to run down from northern BC that [is] going to dump fracking water into the ocean and pollute everything?' You could tell there was a lot of misinformation floating around the community.

Then a young man stood up with passion, and I admired his passion. He said he had been watching our survey boats out in the water, and he believed they were sending out signals and damaging the fish. The company helped explain the work that he had observed and how it was merely survey work that wasn't causing any damage. Nevertheless, you could feel the anger from some… [T]here was a concern that the project was going to destroy the salmon estuary.

I wasn't there when PNW selected the site. The salmon estuary was extremely important and sacred to the locals. It was obvious the site selection caused some problems.

The proponent was getting beat up. The town hall was not going so well. We were getting ready to call it a day, checking our watches and wondering if we were going to make the last ferry or sleep in our cars. Then this elder made his way to the microphone, taking his time, and I recognized him as the person we had spoken with earlier in the day. He gave a speech and you could hear a pin drop while he spoke. He said something like this:

"I've been fishing these waters for the past 80 years, from Alaska down to Saturna. We all remember the days when you could walk on the backs of the salmon. But the salmon are gone, and the LNG isn't here yet. We need to think clearly about the future we want for our children. There haven't been opportunities here for a long time, and our children are moving away in search of jobs. Here we have a company that wants to include us in the process, that is giving us a piece of the pie and wants us to be a part of the environmental protection. We need to listen to what they are saying."

This was a turning point for the project proposal.

That evening in Prince Rupert, all the hereditary chiefs signed a letter of support. Then the project had all the elected chiefs and all the recognized hereditary chiefs.

This all took place after Rich had taken the time to speak with the elder at the rec centre early in the day, and it shows how a small conversation that seems trivial in the moment can actually turn around the dynamic on a $36 billion project. [159]

Coleman worked hard to build a bridge between industry and First Nations because he had spent a lot of time in the northern and remote communities, and he knew how limited the opportunities were.

---

159 Interview with Keivin Hirji, April 21, 2021, by phone.

"LNG is a once-in-a-lifetime opportunity for them to change their economic reality. This is the only resource that is growing in that part of the world. I have heard some of the First Nations chiefs stand up and talk about the need for opportunities for the young people in their communities. It's quite emotional. The training, jobs, and social outcomes in these areas will be significant, and their leaders see this."

Chapter 25
GAMBLING AND CRIME

All media work us over completely. They are so pervasive
in their personal, political, economic, aesthetic, psychological,
moral, ethical, and social consequences that they leave no
part of us untouched, unaffected, unaltered. The medium
is the message. Any understanding of social and cultural
change is impossible without a knowledge of the way media
work as environments. All media are extensions of some
human faculty - psychic or physical.

—Marshall McLuhan,
The Medium is the Massage, 1967

In the many interviews I did of people who knew Coleman or
worked with him, I had a difficult time finding anyone who said
anything negative about him. The strongest criticism was that
he might be loyal to a fault, which was not a criticism around
which I could put a lot of additional description. How, then, did
he become the villain of the story of the end of the BC Liberal
era in government when it came to casinos and allegations of
money laundering?

The NDP began connecting Coleman to money laundering
within weeks of Clark's election as leader of the BC Liberals in
2011. They called on her to fire him before she was even sworn in
as premier, do a full review of gambling in the province, and dump

Rich Coleman as minister in charge of gaming. NDP MLA Shane Simpson claimed Coleman had failed in his job, that gambling was out of control and gaming needed a full review, including illegal money laundering, an investigation into the plans for a large new casino in Vancouver, and gaming grants for charities. The response to this demand to fire Coleman was Coleman dismissing it and saying the government was doing a good job and that a review of money laundering had led to tighter restrictions.[160]

The allegations would increase in frequency and become more extreme in tying Coleman to illegal activities after the 2013 election. Over the years from 2013 until after the 2017 election, the NDP made sure to have Coleman in the crosshairs, when in fact from June 2013 to 2017 Coleman did not have the gaming file.

Meanwhile, Coleman's closest staff were aware that the minister they knew and the one the public thought they knew were very different. Keivan Hirji noted, "I had a number of friends working in developments who knew Rich quite well. Many had seen him on TV, and when I said I was working for him, they always gave me a physical description. They knew he was a very large man, and being deputy premier, they had [a] sense of his importance. He was known to be blunt in the news interviews. I had extended family members who were inherently partisan and encountered some who had a disdain for Rich. I see that as being from the portrayal in the media, rather than knowing who he is."

In January of 2011, Coleman had ordered a report from Rob Kroeker, head of BC's Civil Forfeiture Office, and as a result of Kroeker's recommendations, he oversaw the implementation of several changes in the BC gambling industry, including a move away from cash to electronic funds.

---

160 *NDP wants gaming minister Coleman fired and a review of gambling in B.C.*, *The Canadian Press*, Toronto, ON, March 9, 2011.

"The commitment is to transition the entire industry away from a cash business to an industry that runs on electronic funds transfer," Douglas Scott, head of the Gaming Policy and Enforcement Branch (GPEB), said Wednesday.

Scott said that when British Columbia's casinos first opened, the province felt requiring gamblers to buy chips in cash "would provide a psychological barrier for those people who have a problem with gambling."

But as the sums of money flowing into the province's casinos have grown, they have become a target for organized crime groups seeking to launder illicit funds.

Encouraging patrons to buy chips with wire transfers will create an audit trail going both into and out of the casino.

B.C. Lottery Corp. president Michael Graydon said it has begun experimenting in Metro Vancouver with "gaming accounts" that allow customers to transfer funds from a Canadian bank.[161]

By May of 2015, the issue of money laundering had been connected to the hot Vancouver property market by Geoff Meggs, a councillor with the City of Vancouver who was closely connected to the BC NDP. When the NDP formed government in 2017, Meggs resigned from the City of Vancouver to become chief of staff for Premier John Horgan.

As concern mounts about foreign investment and money laundering in Metro Vancouver, Vision Coun. Geoff Meggs

---

161 *Cash business to be discouraged at B.C. casinos; Move to 'electronic funds' designed to crack down on money laundering*, Chad Skelton, *The Vancouver Sun*, Vancouver, BC, August 25, 2011.

says he believes "there is a really serious" issue in regional housing, but senior governments must initiate any response...

Speaking generally, Meggs said he understands Metro Vancouver residents are increasingly infuriated over foreign investment and the appearance of money laundering in B.C.'s property market.

The Province shared with Meggs information forwarded by a Province reader, from an article recently published by a firm of Chinese-speaking realtors...

"Experts predict that with the increasing strictness of the anti-corruption policies in China, it will continue to cause cash to flow into the Vancouver housing market."

...The firm that published the article claims that 80 per cent of its clients are from Mainland China, and these are the only buyers that can afford to bid currently on homes in Vancouver and West Vancouver. "I do feel that there is a really serious issue that we need to get to the heart of," Meggs said. "I understand people are very concerned about foreign ownership. I think we will need to find measures."

...As for "curbing speculation," he said the provincial government should take the lead because it has most of the taxation "tools that could be brought to bear."

"I wonder if Housing Minister Rich Coleman has thought about foreign ownership," Meggs said. "The province could provide a systemic answer."

A spokeswoman for Coleman said he was not available to interview, and that B.C.'s government believes the responsibility for probing money laundering or taking action on foreign investment falls on federal agencies.[162]

The articles published in the newspapers about money laundering and speculation in the housing market tended to be in the front section of the newspaper and early in the broadcast newscasts. The narrative was gaining momentum, and the BC Liberals were either not responding or replying with denials that there was a serious problem.

In the fall of 2021 while working on a wellness project I met Allan Gregory, who was a battalion chief with Vancouver Fire and Rescue Services (VFRS). He started with VFRS in October of 1992 and served on the union executive for about 10 years, actively engaging in advocacy on behalf of the members, including for recognition of occupational cancer and other related issues. Gregory was active in public relations, spent seven years as secretary treasurer, and helped to create the Vancouver Fire Fighters Charitable Society and other community activities. During this time, he travelled to legislature to meet with MLAs, ministers, and senior staff, engaged in negotiations with the City of Vancouver, and followed current events. His mother was an elected school trustee in Clearbrook, a very small farming town near Kamloops, and he's followed politics for decades although he has not been affiliated with any political party.

While talking to Gregory about wellness, he brought up Coleman as an MLA who advocated for legislation in favour of firefighters. I mentioned that I was writing a book about Coleman. Gregory's tirade about Coleman caught my attention as a route to presenting an objective and informed commentary on how a consumer of current events news in BC perceived Rich Coleman.

---

162 *Who should probe laundering issue?; Meggs says foreign real estate investment a provincial concern; housing minister suggests otherwise*, Sam Cooper, *The Province*, Vancouver, BC, May 10, 2015.

I asked Gregory if he would agree to do two interviews on the record, the first without meeting Rich Coleman and the second at a meeting with Rich Coleman. He agreed to both, and in the interest of an unvarnished presentation, I am sharing his comments here because they reflect what I heard generally from many people in the countdown to the 2017 election.

My perspective developed over time, based on what was happening with the BC Liberal government. His presence alone has an impact. I looked at him as a gentle giant. Any time you heard him speak or when we as firefighters were around him, he was relatively soft-spoken. His presence was big but his voice was not overbearing.

What was interesting about Rich Coleman was watching him over the years he was on TV. He always presented himself well, with a very high degree of confidence, and I think that came from his background as a law enforcement officer. I used to look at him and think he looked like a pretty trustworthy guy and very genuine. He came across that way.

I think that over time, more so under Christy Clark's leadership, he was becoming more of the face of protection of the Liberal government, as opposed to the face of honesty. I'm not saying that I considered him to be dishonest. I mean he was taking a lot of heat for people who were doing or saying some things that the public reacted to, and I think it was strategic that it was done that way because he was a well-respected politician, so he was the spokesperson for the controversies because he could handle himself.

I never saw Rich Coleman get flustered. The media would pepper him like crazy, and he handled it well. I can't remember one time where he became agitated or where you could say, 'Ah, now they've found the wound and they will pour salt on it.' Other politicians, whether in the Liberal party or other parties, would not be able to stay as composed.

I felt badly for him during the years of controversy because he was the one who had to carry all the supplies up Everest.

The Casinogate controversy is where I found that he took a lot for the team. Dude, you could have angel wings on right now and it ain't gonna matter.

He was a good soldier for so long. He was the face of the Liberal party during the casino and money laundering controversies. Everyone wanted Christy's head, and she must have been holed up in some silo somewhere. OK, Rich, you're up, and he handled himself with great composure, but it didn't matter.

Whatever came out of the inquiry, the media stories were damning. He was standing by his man, or at that point his woman, and everyone was wondering how he could keep going when the news stories were so clear that if it walks like a duck and sounds like a duck, it's a duck.

At some point as a government you might have to say, 'There's a problem here and we need to get on top of it.' The problem was they were focused on delete, delete, delete, and deny, deny, deny.

You had two problems here. You had money laundering, and there's no doubt in my mind that the amount of money from Asian markets and organized crime was through the roof, and second you had the transfer tax where the amount of money coming in jumped exponentially. What government isn't going to sit back and say thank you for the extra revenue?

It's one thing to take advantage of higher revenue based on natural resources or economic development, but it's another thing to sit there and not try to counter what everybody else in business, real estate, and other forms of politics are saying: This is out of control.

On top of that, by your lack of action you are almost intentionally and systematically pushing your own people out of the real estate market by allowing the influx of money, especially from Asia. It happened to one of the guys at work. He benefited from what went on a few years ago when he owned a place on a cul-de-sac in Richmond. Realtors of Asian descent would door-knock and say someone wanted to buy the house, then bid the price up until they had a sale.

You are eliminating the ability of your own taxpayers and voters to buy into their own real estate market. They are the people paying for the running of the province; meanwhile, their own government is sitting by while they are priced out of their own market. This forced many of us to move to other parts of the province so that we could own a home.

There was a point where the media confronted Christy. It might have been in the spring—maybe she was looking for her shadow? She denied everything, and by that time the barn door was open and the horse was halfway down the field. Whether it was 100% accurate or not, the public had made up their minds.

I remember the interview with her. I was paying close attention to the issue because there was so much mounting evidence about the problem, especially the real estate issue where people were being interviewed every day about being priced out of the market. The response was all about market demand, as if she had no control. How was that an acceptable answer?

They asked Christy for answers. They presented her with all the evidence and she denied it all. So are we crazy? The media were confused. Were they missing something? I remember she was saying it was not what it seemed, but she didn't offer answers, just denial.

The tentacles that emerged from this one issue were multiple. You get speculation and innuendo. What else is going on? Are there side deals with the Asian buyers? Where does this lead? What does it mean?

The more the government refused to speak to the details of the real estate issue, the more the issue festered.

Then you throw in Casinogate, and the security tapes of people coming into the casino with hockey bags full of money, and it creates a stream of evidence that supports the media stories. Who goes into a casino with $100,000 worth of $20 bills? The big whales at the casinos have other ways to play.

Whether they used that as evidence in the inquiry or not, we as the public can only judge based on the information that we receive, which is from the media. Luckily, we live in a democratic society where there is due process and rules of evidence, but for the public we see what is reported in the news.[163]

---

163 Interview with Allan Gregory, December 12, 2021, by phone.

Coleman was aware that his name became closely connected with money laundering. He had focused on combating organized crime in his early days as solicitor general, with work to combat the rise in influence of the Hells Angels. He knew that gangs in organized crime had lawyers, accountants, and an infrastructure to support their businesses and help them move money locally, regionally, and globally.

"People in the Hells Angels didn't like me because I increased the funds in policing and said we had to go after organized crime. Shortly after, I had a call to my office in Victoria. The guy purported to be a Hells Angel and he told me to be careful because 'we can get you.' The call came through the switchboard so we couldn't trace it. They didn't like that there was a solicitor general who would call them out.

"I funded and was engaged in a $4 million investigation into the Hells Angels and the money problems in Nanaimo. That took down their clubhouse. It was seized and eventually they got it back from the courthouse."[164]

Coleman was not free to talk about a lot of the work he was doing to combat organized crime, and even when the headlines were condemning him, he had a duty to keep much of the information strictly confidential. He admitted that when he took over the gaming file, it was a mess. Two premiers had already been forced to resign over issues related to gaming. He set a goal to create a structure where no politician could interfere with gaming ever again.

"I set up the Gaming Policy Enforcement Branch so that no cabinet minister could interfere. I set it up under the solicitor general. All of the appointees are statutory officers. You can't tell them how to investigate or what to investigate."

When the public narrative came out, there were quotes from

---

164 Interview with Rich Coleman, April 10, 2021, by Zoom.

a senior appointee about the issues. Coleman immediately wondered, "You were the senior investigator on that file. If that's an
issue, why didn't you investigate? That was your job. Why are you
whining about something not being done that was your job?"

Then came the Peter German report, a report that many
people did not read and instead quoted from the executive
summary without challenging the contents. To this day, Coleman
is frustrated about how his information was used or not used in
the conclusions.

"He was in charge of serious crime and he should have been
aware of the need for discretion to protect the safety of some
individuals. He didn't include [that] in his report. In that report,
there's so much hearsay, a little bit of gossip, a little bit of fact, a
whole lot of speculation.

"I will acknowledge I don't remember every discussion, every
briefing note, but the bureaucrat who was in charge of the branch
should remember the information because that was the only job
he had to do. If he can't remember, you have to ask, where were
you? I was in that room that day [and] I can remember the conversation, [so] why can't you?"

After all the controversy, allegations, calls for criminal charges,
and very real impact of the speculation, Coleman has this to
say. "I believe I did my job. I believe other people didn't. And
then they came up with excuses for why they weren't effective.
They had every tool and every dollar to do their job. They were
not underfunded."

Chapter 26
2017 ELECTION

The Liberals were a bit obtuse about where they were after
15 years. There was some fatigue with the voters, and this
left them vulnerable in the 2017 election. I think they were
caught flat-footed. They were left just short of enough votes
to let the NDP with the Greens take over government.
The attack ads in the 2017 campaign were very effective,
with Christy Clark in a crown being showered with money.
The NDP spent all their money on these ads. The NDP
campaign left the impression of a soiled government, not
taking money laundering seriously enough.

—Keith Baldrey, Global BC Legislative
Bureau Chief, December 7, 2023

The BC Liberals went into the 2017 general election with a well-funded election machine, a slate of first-rate candidates, an experienced campaign team, and a platform to govern the province with a surplus budget. They were aiming for their fifth consecutive general election win.

Keith Baldrey observed that there was a disconnect between the BC Liberals and the voters. "The problem with Christy's government [was] they developed a sense of bulletproofitis. 'We're unbeatable, we were supposed to lose in 2013, and we won, we don't have to worry.'"[165]

He recalls a meeting that occurred shortly before the election when Finance Minister Mike de Jong called the media into a conference to set the stage for the election messages. De Jong proudly announced that the BC Liberals would be campaigning in the election with a $2.9 billion surplus that they planned to use to pay down the provincial debt. Baldrey was thinking, "Are you nuts? The affordability issue was already there. People were looking for relief, and instead of giving any of it back you are going to put it against a debt no one knew existed?"

The contrast with the NDP election message was clear. "They announce[d] they [would] get rid of bridge tolls, and boom, suddenly ridings in Surrey and elsewhere became winnable."

A government that has been in power for a long time can often lose touch with people who can provide some independent perspective. If a government develops a "siege" mentality where they see voters are either supporters or enemies, then independent messages have a hard time reaching them because there are too many gatekeepers. Baldrey explained, "When you are in government for 16 years, you lose track of where you are in government. The NDP will have the same issue if they win the next election. You have to be able to renew yourself. You can't get used to being in government."[166]

Christy Clark knew from decades of experience in and out of politics and the media that crafting the right message is not always easy. "How do we make sure the budget is balanced and at the same time minimize the surplus we are going to end up with? It's a guessing game because you never know how much money you will have. You don't want to have too big a surplus. You want it to be in people's pockets. It's a balancing act and the numbers evolve over time as you see how your policy is impacting revenue.

165 Interview with Keith Baldrey, December 7, 2023, by Zoom.
166 Interview with Keith Baldrey, ibid.

"If you want to have enough money to build a hospital some-where, you want to carve that out in advance. That's in the capital budget and you have to plan it. If you want to have enough money to pay for more drugs in the subsidized budget, that's a program expenditure and you can do that closer to budget day.

"Once you've been in government for a while, there's continu-ity there. Your message is, 'Let us keep doing what we are doing,' as opposed to the message of radical change."[167]

Meanwhile, Coleman's provincial image had suffered going into the election. Baldrey noted, "Over time, he began to wear some of the problems the BC Liberals brought on to them-selves, like money laundering and corporate political donations. The NDP pinned all of this on Coleman, that somehow he was complicit in everything negative that was going on. They really hung a lot on Christy, and Rich as well. He became public enemy number 2.

"It started under Campbell, even though Campbell was really controlling, so it was hard for ministers to shine or punch above their weight. Christy Clark had a really decentralized approach, she was only interested in issues she was interested in…This meant her ministers could create their own profile, and Rich emerged as the voice of her government."

While Clark's government was governing, the BC Liberals were ready for the campaign. Coleman co-chaired the election campaign committee, put the key people in place, and guided the work. As per his previous campaigns, it was an effective team and strategy. Clark also gave credit to Coleman for the fundraising. "Rich was a very successful fundraiser because he was excellent at networking. He made them feel special. An elderly couple donating $35 was just as important as the business supporter at the big dinners."

---

167 Interview with Christy Clark, June 2, 2021, by Zoom.

The BC Liberals won a minority government, losing the majority by 1 seat. In fact, it is my observation that if Don McRae had run for re-election in the riding of Courtenay–Comox, Christy Clark would have won a second majority government. Instead, McRae announced his plans to retire from politics in 2016. Jim Benninger, a former base commander of CFB Comox, ran for the BC Liberals. On election night, he had lost by nine votes. After a three-day recount including the absentee votes, he lost the seat by 189 votes and Christy Clark had a minority government. The BC Liberals won 44 seats, the NDP won 41 seats, and the Green Party made history by electing 3 MLAs under the leadership of Dr. Andrew Weaver, a well-respected MLA from Victoria who had previously worked as a professor at the University of Victoria. Weaver was well known for his decades of work on climate change science.

A key point that seemed to be missed in the aftermath of the election was that Christy Clark had actually won the election. The NDP and Green Party made sure they stayed on message in all the social media interactions that I witnessed and only referred to the BC Liberals loss. In fact, any time someone tried to point out that Christy Clark had won, there were comments by NDP and Green supporters that this was sour grapes. It was a very consistent and effective strategy because the narrative stuck. I know this because I did try many times to correct the narrative and was told I was just sticking up for the BC Liberals. Anyone who has followed anything I have said for decades will know that in fact I was just wanting to make sure the conversation was accurate.

Another key point that has to be put on the public record is that Christy Clark made history by becoming the first woman in Canada, and likely in most democratic jurisdictions around the world, to win two general elections. The fact that the second government she won was a minority is actually not relevant to the fact that she won the election. At the time of the writing of this book,

Justin Trudeau is governing Canada with a minority government, and I have yet to see anyone say he lost the last general election.

However, this book is about Rich Coleman and the BC Liberals' time in power, not about the ongoing misogyny of politics, and it is important to dive into what was reported, what happened with the 2017 election, and what happened next. In some ways, it all revolves around rugby and beer.

I first met Dr. Andrew Weaver when he was the rugby coach for my boyfriend, and the older brother of my boyfriend's best friend, when I was 16. Rugby was a real passion for Weaver then, and it remained a passion through the decades. I reconnected with Weaver when I was hosting a TV show in Victoria and he was a professor at the University of Victoria. I found it iconic to Weaver's personality that the deal made to bring down the Christy Clark government was made at a rugby match near Victoria.

> NDP leader John Horgan and Green Party boss Andrew Weaver insisted that politics wasn't on the agenda as they cheered on Canada in a losing cause against New Zealand in the finals of the HSBC World Rugby Women's Sevens Series event.

> Weaver said he saw Horgan in the crowd and the two decided to sit together, however, he also noted that he'd be meeting with the Liberal party later in the evening.

> On Friday Weaver said he was "very close" to making a deal with either the Liberals or the New Democrats on forming a new minority government.[168]

In fact, there was little discussion between the Greens and the BC Liberals. Soon after that match, Horgan and Weaver

---

168 *ElxnBC-Rugby, The Canadian Press*, Toronto, ON, May 28, 2017.

announced that the Green Party would be supporting the NDP in the BC Legislature and would vote against the BC Liberals on the next confidence motion. It was a dramatic time, and all eyes were on the legislature as the story played out.

> The BC Liberals have been defeated on a vote of confidence, leaving the province's Lieutenant-Governor to decide whether to call a snap election or invite the NDP to form a fragile government requiring the support of the Green Party... when the vote of confidence on Ms. Clark's free-spending Throne Speech was called on Thursday evening, those Green and NDP MLAs on the other side of the House stood together and voted her government down.
>
> A hush fell over the packed House as the roll call was read.
>
> Afterward, Ms. Clark emerged from the chamber to applause from staff, MLAs and other supporters who lined the halls.
>
> Inside the legislature, NDP Leader John Horgan embraced former NDP leader Carole James in a bear hug. In the floor seats behind his caucus were retired NDP cabinet ministers Moe Sihota and Sue Hammell...
>
> It was Ms. Guichon's unusual task to decide what comes next for British Columbia's government. The NDP and Greens had earlier delivered a statement to the Lieutenant-Governor, advising that they had signed an accord that promised stability under a minority NDP government.[169]

---

169 *Confidence vote brings down BC Liberals: Christy Clark fails to gain support of NDP or Green parties, despite delivering a Throne Speech packed with opposition policies*, Mike Hager and Justine Hunter, *The Globe and Mail*, Toronto, ON, June 30, 2017.

There was a lot of talk in BC about what would happen next. Because BC's politics has been so polarized for most of BC's history, there were no modern precedents for minority governments. Politics in BC was a zero-sum game at election time. This plot twist required a lot of education of the voters about the options, and the very close numbers of seats meant the math still did not work for the NDP.

Why was the math still not working? The NDP had won 41 seats, so even with the three MLAs from the Green Party supporting them on confidence matters, they were only at 44 seats. The BC Liberals had won 43 seats and the NDP had to give up one MLA to the position of Speaker. This put the numbers at an even 43 to 43 on any confidence votes. While it is true that the Speaker could and would break a tie in the favour of the NDP, there was one more issue. Most of the work of the legislature occurs at Committee. At Committee, the Speaker retires and the Deputy Speaker takes the Chair. With a Deputy Speaker in the Chair, the NDP vote reduces to 42 and the BC Liberal vote wins with 43.

It seemed inevitable that the lieutenant governor would have to call another election in order to have a legislature in BC that was functioning. There was more speculation in the media about what would and could happen next, and a lot of commentary on what had happened. One of the harshest criticisms of Clark was in Coleman's local paper.

> Christy Clark, formerly premier of B.C., has not had a good year.

> But it's kind of hard to feel sorry for her. Her wounds have been self-inflicted.

> Clark and the B.C. Liberals were in the best possible position to win another majority.

Unemployment is low and the provincial coffers are stuffed.

That led to Clark's first mistake – she ran a campaign based on the idea that we ought to be grateful for how good things were going.

No one fretting over stagnant wages or impossible housing prices wanted to hear that…

But do you replace Clark now, when a single NDP misstep could trigger a new election? Who would lead the Liberals? Or do you keep her, even knowing she's burned her bridges with the electorate? The Liberals are between a rock and a Clark place.[170]

Many people were watching on television when Premier Christy Clark walked up the steps of Government House in Victoria, BC, to speak with Lieutenant Governor Judith Guichon to discuss the options available after the BC Liberals had lost the confidence vote. Because the math in the legislature did not work, Clark felt it was reasonable to ask for another election, even though she had previously been opposed to that. Clark and Horgan were both very discreet about the discussion that they each had with the lieutenant governor. Both discussions took place on the evening of June 29, with all onlookers standing by, wondering which leader would end up in power. Clark's meeting lasted for over an hour. Horgan arrived shortly after, and about 20 minutes later he left the meeting knowing he would be the next premier, with an incredibly narrow majority cobbled together through a coalition with the Green Party MLAs—and complicity from one BC Liberal MLA, as would be revealed later. As legislative reporter

---

170 *Self-inflicted injuries dog Liberals*, Matthew Claxton, *Langley Advance*, Langley, BC, July 6, 2017.

Mike Smyth observed:

> Clark will be a fierce opposition force against an untested NDP government. Horgan's cabinet would be full of rookies and mistakes would undoubtedly be made.
>
> The Liberal opposition, meanwhile, will be the biggest in B.C. history and made up of former cabinet ministers who know their portfolios cold.
>
> As one Liberal insider said to me: "It would be the weakest government in B.C. history against the strongest Opposition in B.C. history."[171]

---

171 *B.C. politics: Fitting for a TV soap opera*, Mike Smyth, *The Province*; Vancouver, BC, June 30, 2017.

Chapter 27
THE FALL OF THE BC LIBERALS

May's cliffhanger election finally ended 52 days later when Liberal premier Christy Clark gave a throne speech that read like a deathbed conversion but Andrew Weaver still gave John Horgan his rose (wait, no, that was The Bachelor*). Then Clark disappeared into an alternate dimension (wait, no, that was* Stranger Things*). Then Darryl Plecas became speaker, at which point Rich Coleman flew out of the rafters and roasted him with flaming dragon's breath (wait, no, that was* Game of Thrones*.)*[172]

—Jack Knox, *Times-Colonist*, September 10, 2017

Hindsight, as they say, is 20/20. After the election, Christy Clark noted, "Rich was really important to the 2017 campaign. He was steering the ship. In retrospect, given that Rich's advice wasn't being heard by senior leadership, we should have sent him out door-to-door in the ridings where we could see it was a close race. There's nobody better than Rich at going door-to-door. As we neared the end of the campaign, we knew there were a lot of close races."

---

172 *Summer's over. Here's what you missed,* Jack Knox, *Times-Colonist,* Victoria, BC, September 10, 2017.

What happened when Christy Clark walked into Government House? What did she discuss with the lieutenant governor? Clark shared the scene. "After intense work, we delivered our Throne Speech. I remember Moe Sihota looking at me with real sympathy, shaking his head, and I felt he knew something that I didn't know about how it was all going to turn out.

"Then I went to see the lieutenant governor and she had made up her mind to give the NDP a chance. It didn't make sense. The constitutional precedent wasn't there. So I figured she knew something that I didn't know."

It became obvious later that in fact the lieutenant governor had learned from a BC Liberal MLA that he was planning to prop up the NDP–Green coalition by accepting the position of Speaker. This meant that the math, in fact, did work by the narrowest of margins. In this instance, the lieutenant governor had a duty to invite the coalition to govern.

Clark continued, "When I went to visit her, she ordered a couple of glasses of wine, and when the wine came, she started telling me how she went to visit a fortune teller. The fortune teller told her the name of the man she was going to marry, and how she was going to be on the stage, and now that she is lieutenant governor, she was on the stage. So what the fortune teller had told her had come true.

"I remember thinking, 'This is a very odd moment in BC history between the premier and the lieutenant governor.'"[173]

Why did the lieutenant governor ask John Horgan and the NDP–Green coalition to form government when there was still an issue with the seats? The answer came in the form of a partisan move where BC Liberal Daryl Plecas accepted the position of Speaker of the Legislature, allowing the NDP–Greens to be able to pass legislation in committee with the deputy Speaker breaking any tie votes if needed.

---

173 Interview with Christy Clark, June 2, 2021, by Zoom.

After the BC Liberals lost the confidence vote, there was a big meeting in Penticton. The BC Liberals were not sure what would happen next, or how stable the NDP–Green coalition would be. Clark recalled, "Rich went around to the caucus and everyone signed a document that they would not run for speaker, except for Plecas who was having some kind of problem. Plecas blew off some steam and then left the meeting. I think I misjudged the room because I said, 'Let's not dump on him, let's move on.'

"We had a caucus with a lot of people in it who had never been in politics before and we had some people in the room who understood how hard politics was, who knew that changing a leader is something that needs to be done very thoughtfully and very carefully. Those folks were very clear in their views and were very passionate in supporting me. Rich and Shirley both stood out for their passion. Then there were others who just didn't know any better. They had never been in opposition, or they were newly elected, or some… were ambitious and wanted to see a leadership race.

"I looked around the room and I listened to them, and I probably could have stayed and fought. But I didn't want to stay. It was against my better judgement. My only regret is that I didn't make the decision before that."[174]

Christy Clark announced her resignation as leader of the BC Liberals from Penticton on July 28, 2017. She had served as premier for six-and-a-half years.

> "…a leader should know when it's her time to leave. I just don't admire people who hang on because they believe they are irreplaceable. Because nobody is irreplaceable.

> "(The BC Liberals) were grieving… And what they need is they need a leadership campaign to refresh and energize and get everybody thinking about what's next."

---

174 Interview with Christy Clark, ibid.

..."The night the lieutenant governor decided not to call an election I was going to go out and tell [the media] that I was going to step down, but I was persuaded not to do that," she said. "There's a good time to go and a bad time to go and that would have been a bad time to go...

"It's also become clear, said Clark, that Green leader Andrew Weaver is more committed to propping up the new NDP government than she'd thought, dashing hopes for a quick election.

"I think I did underestimate Andrew Weaver's willingness to go along to get along," she said. "He's really decided he wants to be a part of the NDP... and that has really given the new government a lot more stability because there doesn't seem to be anything they can do to throw a wrench into that relationship.

"Given we're not likely to have an election, now is the time to have a leadership (race)."[175]

Christy Clark left the caucus to their deliberations the day after she announced her resignation as leader. The meeting continued, and before the end of the meeting, Rich Coleman had been selected as the interim leader of the BC Liberal Party.

"Most fun I ever had in politics was working with Christy Clark. Not only did she give me a great job and a lot of respect, [but] it was wonderful to watch her grow into the position. It was a fun movie to watch. She did an amazing job." Coleman spoke with Clark after he became interim leader. "She called me and I asked her how she was doing. I said to her, 'I told you I

---

175   *Clark knew it was 'her time to leave'; Moving On,* Rob Shaw, *The Province,* Vancouver, BC, August 1, 2017.

wanted you to stay and you left.' She replied, 'Coleman, you've been cleaning up my fucking messes for years, and now you're cleaning up my last one.'"

Chapter 28
LEADERSHIP

A leader is best when people barely know he exists, when his work is done, his aim fulfilled, they will say: we did it ourselves.

—Lao Tzu, c. 500 BC

After many years of rising through the ranks of political leadership, Rich Coleman was leader of the BC Liberal Party. It carried the word "interim" with it. He said the worst meeting he ever attended in his life was the one where Daryl Plecas went after Christy Clark in the caucus meeting, and the next day, he became leader of the party.

"The treatment of Daryl Plecas to Christy was egregious, and I told him so. There were not a lot of people jumping up to support her. I think that hurt her more than anything. I saw her at lunch... [and] said we can get through this. I know she talked to a lot of people, but she decided to leave the next day.

"After she left, I looked around the caucus and thought how dysfunctional it all was, so I left, took a walk, tried to figure out what to do. Michele was camping. I couldn't get hold of her."

Coleman was mulling over whether or not he should accept the position of interim leader. It had been a rollercoaster of change and uncertainty in the previous two months, coming off an intense political campaign.

"[West Vancouver MLA] Ralph Sultan stood up and said there is only one guy who can take over as interim leader. So a bunch of people stood up and said, 'If you take on interim leader, you can't run for leader unless you step aside from that role.'"

Why did they say if he was interim leader he couldn't run for leader? What if he had said, "OK, then, I will not take the interim position?" What would have happened if later, he had said, "I changed my mind, I'm going to run?" He would never go back on his word, although others would and have done so in similar situations. We will never know the answer to those questions. What we do know is that he said yes and took on the job of interim leader of the BC Liberal Party.

When Coleman talked about how it came about, it was possible to hear the frustration rising again, as if he were second-guessing his decision. "Stupid loyalty is that I took on the position of interim leader. I found out after I took over that I had no staff. They had all taken severance and left."

Everything was complete chaos when Coleman took over. His Chief of Staff Toby Myers was one of the many automatic terminations because she had been appointed by order in Council, so the transition severed the appointment. He drove Myers to Sunshine Valley—she was heading on to Penticton from there—and on the drive convinced her to come back to work as chief of staff for the Opposition Caucus.

Coleman had been driving to Sunshine Valley because Michele and the kids were camping there. He remembered that when he pulled in, Michele said, "What have you done now?"

Michele already knew that Coleman had taken the position of interim leader because their daughter Jacqueline had a flat tire on the way to Sunshine Valley and had to stop in Hope, where it was on the news. His granddaughter saw him on television and asked her mother what an interim leader was, and that is how his family found out even while on a camping trip.

When Coleman returned to the legislature on the Sunday before work resumed, he saw how difficult his job would be. "I went into the legislature. There was nothing—no computers, no telephones. I had no office assigned to me." He walked through the debris from the move to the opposition offices and realized there was absolutely no strategy in place for what the BC Liberals were facing.

"I had to write a business plan for the caucus. By the end of the week I had people hired. They had to make a decision by 5:00 p.m. By the following Monday, I had the offices sorted out. I also set up a tour of the legislature for all the MLAs and their families [and] gave all the MLAs briefing packages. We had copies of the transition binders. I gave them orientation including practice Question Period. They were all new to opposition except for Linda Reid, Mike de Jong, and myself."

Mike Morris remembered the transition. "He was very good as interim leader, very approachable. I was going through some things at the time and was able to talk them through.

"When he became interim leader, there was a lot of discussion with signs of emerging discord. When he let his name stand, he had to agree that he would not let his name stand for leader. When Christy stepped down suddenly, there was a lot of emotion and I think he felt it was necessary that based on his tenure, his connections, and experience, he needed to help hold things together. This meant he disqualified himself from running. He was a very good lieutenant to have at your side.

"He is a very imposing individual. He has quite a stature to him. He's been around for a while. And probably the cop showed up every once in a while. He was well suited for the role of interim leader."[176]

Coleman wanted Keivan Hirji to stay and help with the BC Liberal opposition, and he also said yes. "He wanted to build a

---

176 Interview with Mike Morris, April 22, 2021, by Zoom.

functioning opposition organization structure that the new leader could walk into and have a well-oiled machine. His goal as opposition leader was to prepare it for the next leader and keep the ship pointing straight. The role of the party leader and the opposition leader are very different, and the constitution of the party does not anticipate 'interim leadership.'"

There was a significant contrast between government and opposition. Hirji remembers what it was like after Clark resigned and Coleman took over. "Staff were shaken up. They had just finished a period of uncertainty after the election, then they were in opposition, and then there was an interim leader. The first thing that Rich did was call a full staff meeting.

"Legislative staff had to rearrange the caucus room because they had never had an opposition that was so big. The reorganization had to be with a bunch of long tables, like the kind you [would] set up if you were handing out food at an event. Rich had it set up into a big rectangular donut. He said he recognized we had been through a lot and the staff had been through a lot, and that his goal was to bring in some stability and build an effective opposition organization, which serves the very important role of accountability in a parliamentary system. He said that they were all tasked with working together to bring in a new, stable structure, and that he would have an open-door policy. I think a lot of staff took him up on that. I saw a lot of staff walking through his door just to talk to him."

An open-door policy for any leader is extremely rare. Leaders, whether interim or otherwise, generally have gatekeepers and layers of staff between them and other staff or certain MLAs. In politics, leaders often govern with a lot of ego and try to hoard power. Coleman was atypical and led the opposition the way he had led his ministries: He created systems, identified talent, empowered talent, analysed resources, created strategies to deploy the resources, wrote out plans, assigned tasks, and led execution.

Hirji said, "The way he managed the caucus, he recognized his role as being the leader of the opposition, as well as the person who needed to give a lot of profile to the MLAs. For example, in the premier's estimates, Rich made sure that any MLA who wanted to ask a question of the premier would have a chance to do that in the premier's estimates. This was a major departure from the norm. I think we had about 20 or so MLAs asking the premier questions."[177]

Vancouver–Quilchena MLA Andrew Wilkinson won the leadership and replaced Christy Clark on the fifth ballot of the leadership convention vote on February 3, 2018. He became Leader of the official opposition and led the BC Liberals in the general election held on October 24, 2020. The BC Liberals had the worst election outcome that they had experienced as BC Liberals, and the lowest seat count since the return to the legislature of Liberal MLAs in 1991. Coleman announced his intention to not seek re-election in the 2020 election in February of the same year, and his riding was won by NDP Megan Dykeman.

177 Interview with Keivan Hirji, April 21, 2021.

Chapter 29
THE CULLEN COMMISSION

I think fundamentally the allegation of money laundering was part of a racist agenda. I don't think the NDP's big idea was to try and stir up racism, I just think they found that playing to people's worst instincts about immigrants was something they were willing to do in order to pursue their agenda. The NDP started there: 'The Chinese are stealing our jobs.' They moved on to: 'The Chinese are bringing over dirty money and buying luxury cars.' Then it was all about inflating the price of houses, and it moved to money laundering. People wonder why Vancouver has so much anti-Asian hatred and underlying violence. It was all building up over time and it started with this political agenda to target the Chinese to get votes. David Eby did a study with Andy Yan and the sample size was very small and they concluded that it was Asian buyers. They did that by looking at the last name of the owner. Guess what? It turns out that as we started tracking foreign buyers it was Americans, Indians, Koreans, Iranians. And the money laundering? The commission investigated and there was nothing there.

—Christy Clark, Interview, June 2, 2021

In May of 2019, the NDP government launched a full investigation into money laundering. Called the Cullen Commission, it was led by British Columbia Supreme Court Justice Austin Cullen and mandated to report on:

- the extent and methods of money laundering in BC;

- the acts or omissions of various regulatory agencies and public institutions that contribute to money laundering in the province;

- the effectiveness of anti-money laundering efforts by these agencies and individuals; and,

- the current barriers to effective law enforcement in this area.

After three reports were published on money laundering, the NDP launched the Cullen Commission.

The day began with the BC NDP announcing the political agenda for the inquiry into money laundering, even before John Horgan and his ministers had gotten around to rubber stamping the terms of reference. The NDP posted a link on their social media to a website entitled "the B.C. Liberal decade of dirty money" at 8:30 a.m. that day. Two hours later, Premier Horgan met with reporters to officially announce the inquiry. There was a large mandate for the commission, and two years given to it to work through its list of responsibilities. Horgan pointed to the previous work done by the provincial panel and by Peter German as the foundation for the inquiry's work.

But was the commissioner, B.C. Supreme Court Justice Austin Cullen, bound by the NDP's two-year political schedule? No, not really, though it took several questions before Horgan conceded as much...

Last time the New Democrats appointed a public inquiry – into the Nanaimo bingo scandal back in 1996 – it needed a half dozen extensions over five years. The inquiry was still stumbling along when the B.C. Liberals took office and put it out of its misery.[178] Coleman was in the crosshairs of the NDP on this issue and had been for years. They were clear that their goal was to throw all the resources of government into an inquiry that would prove, once and for all, that the allegations of criminal money laundering leading to a lack of housing affordability were true, and that the BC Liberals were complicit, with Coleman as the leader of all the bad deeds.

As Vaughn Palmer wrote about six months after Premier Horgan's launch of the inquiry, Justice Cullen wanted to manage the expectations of the final outcome.

When the money-laundering inquiry held a public meeting in the provincial capital this week, commissioner Austin Cullen opened with some cautionary remarks about what his mandate does and does not entail.

One bears repeating, in light of over-the-top expectations in some quarters that the commission will be identifying perpetrators of the crime of money laundering and then meting out the appropriate punishment. "It is important to be aware that the powers of the commission are set out in the Public Inquiry Act which does not permit me to make findings of criminal guilt or civil liability, or to impose punishment or award any kind of remedy," said Cullen in addressing the three dozen or so members of the public gathered in the ballroom of a downtown Victoria hotel Monday night.

Rather, "the terms of reference specifically require me to forward any information obtained during the inquiry

178 *Money-launder inquiry is aimed at liberals*, Vaughn Palmer, *The Vancouver Sun*, Vancouver, BC, May 16, 2019.

that may be useful in the investigation or prosecution of a criminal offence to the appropriate authorities," said the B.C. Supreme Court Justice.

So in terms of the prospects for crime and punishment: maybe, maybe not, and in any event, not likely within the remaining 18 months' time frame for the inquiry, which is obliged by the NDP government to deliver a final report in May 2021.[179]

Every notable name associated with the controversies over the years was called to testify. The hearings were televised and posted online. The reports were published online. Lawyers, advocates, interest groups, political players, and business people were involved and following the process. It was an enormous undertaking. Though the commission was mandated to report out in May 2021, the final report was actually released on June 22, 2022. This book was started with an expectation to be finished in the fall of 2021 and was delayed pending the outcome of the report and the aftermath of the political shifts occurring.

While the report in its thoroughness did in fact make many detailed recommendations and have many specific findings, there was no damning finding of Coleman or Clark other than that they could have done more. In fact, the federal agency FINTRAC came out as one of the most negligent government agencies, and there was a list of recommendations for this and many other agencies. Cullen also listed all the economic sectors where there might be a connection to money laundering.

The key message of the Report is clear and unequivocal: money laundering is a significant issue in British Columbia

---

179 *Inquiry for coming clean on money laundering has limits, challenges,* Vaughn Palmer, *The Vancouver Sun,* Vancouver, BC, November 7, 2019.

and more regulatory oversight is required to tackle the problem. While the Cullen Commission did not provide a specific number on the amount of illicit funds that are laundered through the BC economy each year, they estimated that it is within the realm of billions of dollars per year.

While the resulting action of governments in the wake of this Report remains to be seen, its release puts direct pressure on the BC Government to establish further regulatory oversight and enforcement that may affect the industries that are targeted by money laundering. The Report also indicates that there are significant failures within FINTRAC, the federal agency responsible for money laundering, which implicates further regulatory tightening that must occur at a federal level.[180]

So much of the noise surrounding the investigation of criminal activity connected to money laundering rolled out in a series of reports prior to the Cullen Commission. Most notable were two reports written by a former deputy commissioner of the RCMP, Peter German. Frequently referred to as "The German Report" they were actually called *Dirty Money: an Independent Review of Money Laundering in Lower Mainland Casinos* and *Dirty Money: an Independent Review of Money Laundering in B.C. Real Estate, Luxury Vehicle Sales & Horse Racing*. The first was released on March 18, 2018 and the second on March 31, 2019. They were both high-profile and controversial, and the NDP made good use of the findings to go after Coleman repeatedly.

At the time that "The German Report" was published, Coleman was in opposition and Andrew Wilkinson was leader

180 *The Cullen Commission Overview, Dentons,* July 19, 2022. https://www.dentons.com/en/insights/articles/2022/july/14/the-cullen-commission-overview

of the BC Liberals. Coleman was incredibly frustrated that the strategy of the BC Liberals was to say nothing in response to the report.

Coleman said, "The guy who wanted to push back on 'The German Report' was Mike Morris, but the caucus wouldn't let him. So we said nothing. Many people had not even read the reports—they just saw the headlines over and over. There were accusations in German's report that people could come in and pay $250,000 to buy a luxury car. That's technically illegal. My objection to that is if you had this in your report, did you report it to the police? Because if a bank took that money from the dealer, they broke the law. If you have this, I hope you gave it to someone to investigate. I'm sure he didn't. He detailed it pretty well in his report.

"When I read 'The German Report' I was on the ferry, heading back from Victoria. So he's basically saying $10 million per year was being laundered in the casinos for ten years, but I know the gaming revenue was $2 billion per year and it made $1.1 billion for government. So I'm thinking—this isn't a big number in terms of percentage. He didn't even address the fact that he was a former police officer, so why not admit that these things were being investigated. You read it, and you read it again, and you realize that there's no factual data behind it. It's just a narrative."

While Morris and Coleman wanted to fight back against the contents of the report, the rest of the caucus was afraid. "[I] kept saying, 'What are we afraid of?' We need[ed] to be able to call BS on it, but they wouldn't. So the party, particularly Wilkinson, did nothing. Why are you just throwing us under the bus? They had no jam.

"I think because Wilkinson thought he was the 'new clean guy.'"

Coleman knew the BC Liberals were not perfect, and he admitted they made mistakes, but there were a lot of statements in the two reports that he thought would have been easily dispelled. Instead they provided traction to the NDP to launch the full inquiry.

"Is it possible that German made it up? I would like to think he didn't. He had a lot of information in the report. Nothing has been done about it. The report came out over two years ago."

Coleman and Morris wanted to hold the NDP to task for the contents of "The German Report," but Wilkinson and the caucus strategists did not want to be connected to any discussions of the contents of the reports. Meanwhile, the publicity around the reports set a narrative that helped to validate the need for the Cullen Commission, and Coleman knew that when he was called to testify, he was going to be asked about many areas that had not been part of his mandate at any time.

In his life, Coleman had been responsible for many different issues, from the time he was an RCMP officer, through his years as a business owner and his many years in government in key portfolios. He had not experienced a situation before where he was feeling guilty until proven innocent by a tribunal, a quasi-judicial review process. The stress was extreme, and he had many months of anxiety, not knowing what he would be asked to be accountable for, based on what he had read in German's reports.

"I couldn't give any testimony on the real estate issue. The only housing I did was care home and affordable housing. Real estate was always with the ministry of finance. The Commission is supposed to go through luxury cars and real estate after it finishes with gaming.

"My lawyer estimates that with the lottery portion alone it would be a million dollars in legal fees. We didn't know how long it would take to come out with the report. Every aspect of the commission was covered by indemnities for the legal costs."

The anxiety of the uncertainty was significant. At the time that Coleman decided not to run again, after 24 years of public service, he was under the cloud of a major inquiry as the key target. The words "organized crime," "money laundering," and "luxury real estate" were all connected to him, as if he were a high-flying criminal. Coleman lives in a modest house in a Langley subdivision and drives a truck. Both are very nice, and both are affordable to any Canadian family where someone is earning well. There's nothing luxurious about his lifestyle.

How much time did he have to spend on the Cullen Commission? Coleman reads everything, and so just to go through the directly relevant testimony took him over 40 hours.

"It interrupts your flow. You have to deal with communications from your lawyer. I wanted to get it behind me because then I could focus on other things and [wouldn't] have to worry about what happens next in this. When I see an email from my lawyer that he is going to meet with Kash Heed and his lawyer, that just plays on my mind. Falcon messages me because he sees my photo on the news with Christy and other ministers and says not to worry, I will kick this. Meanwhile I'm losing sleep because I don't know what kind of salacious things Heed might say. Or when I read Fred Pennick commenting about me squeezing his hand until it hurts. My statement is, 'It never happened.' Fred Pennick is not a tiny guy. He's an ex-cop.

"It causes angst."

The statement Coleman is referring to is actually one reason I decided to write this book. As I said at the very beginning, I did not know him as a person. However, I remember the media stories in December of 2020 when former police officer Fred Pennick was quoted in the news that Rich Coleman intimidated him at a reception because when they shook hands, Coleman squeezed his hand until it hurt. When I heard that on the news, I actually laughed out loud.

I may not have known Coleman well, but I did know two things: That was not a credible statement of what might have happened, and Fred Pennick was a rare man to publicly say that another man had hurt his hand in a handshake. It seemed beyond absurd for any man to say, 'That man bullied me in public with a handshake,' and for that to be a major news story.

When I spoke with Coleman about a month later, he was very upset about the years of publicity, and that statement really bothered him. I told him that the statement had made me laugh.

After all of the time and money and anxiety over the Cullen Commission, when the final report was published, Justice Cullen did a good and thorough job of recommending improvements for federal and provincial agencies. Vaughn Palmer said the NDP hoped for much more out of the report. "As a scandal, it was a bit of a flop. The final report was critical of Coleman. I think the criticisms were fair. He really didn't face the evidence that was mounting that money laundering was real. He should have done more as the top cop."

"The taxpayers of BC have spent tens of millions of dollars over the past three years for this inquiry, and the conclusion is that we were all doing our jobs, and doing them as well as we could in difficult circumstances," Coleman said. "As the NDP is learning, government is complicated, and the information received by ministers can often conflict with each other. But slinging mud at the professionals and public servants doing their best on behalf of the people of BC is not in anyone's interest."[181]

As Cullen laid out in his report:

> "[No elected officials] knowingly encouraged, facilitated, or permitted money laundering to occur in order to obtain personal benefit or advantage, be it financial, political, or otherwise... after a thorough inquiry, I found no evidence of corruption."[182]

---

181 Interview with Vaughn Palmer, December 6, 2023, by Zoom.

182 *Cullen Commission Final Report,* June 12, 2022, Commission of Inquiry into Money Laundering in British Columbia, Province of British Columbia.

"The word corruption has been tossed around irresponsibly by media and politicians for several years, but the Commissioner has found that to be utterly false," said Coleman. "While hindsight is 20/20 and there is always more that could have been done, the idea that we were somehow purposefully ignoring or somehow aiding money laundering has been proven to be incorrect."

In his final report, Commissioner Cullen noted that Coleman received different advice from different branches of the public service, and that Coleman did the right thing by engaging an independent expert, Robert Kroeker, to review the differing information he was given.

"The Commissioner has reinforced clearly that this decision was, as he wrote, 'prudent and appropriate,'" said Coleman. "The Commission's toughest criticism was for federal law enforcement and specifically FINTRAC, concerns I share."

Palmer followed the progress of the entire issue, and he knew that the NDP were hoping for serious damage to Coleman. They really wanted to have the enquiry result in criminal charges. "They were hoping in particular that it would damage Coleman, that they would find evidence that would lead to criminal charges. They had a platoon of lawyers, access to documentation you and I [couldn't] even dream of. All they could say was he could have done more. They didn't find corruption."

Keith Baldrey said he was never convinced that the Cullen Commission would find anything serious. "The NDP thought Coleman was going to be nailed by the Cullen Commission. I never shared that point of view given Coleman's confident handling of the issue. I do think he should have taken it more seriously or prevent[ed] it from getting as big as it did."

He thought the real issue was the handling of the situation by the BC Liberals. "The problem for the Liberals is that Coleman kept dismissing it as [a non-]issue, so it left the impression that the government didn't care about an issue that mattered to the voters.

The publicity around Cullen and the related controversies had everyone feeling the government was really damaged goods.

"The image of hockey bags full of cash was really dramatic."

As for the issue of housing affordability, Baldrey believes the BC Liberals allowed the NDP opposition to hammer them with that issue until it felt like it was true. "There was evidence of foreign investment in Vancouver and housing prices, but it didn't explain the cost of housing in Kelowna or other parts of the province. There were many other factors contributing to housing costs, why did my house go from $250,000 to $1.5 million in Victoria? It wasn't money laundering.

"Rich and Christy never took it seriously enough. They could have hit back, but they didn't.

"The housing issue continues to devil the government to this day, so clearly it wasn't the fault of the BC Liberal government. It was a much bigger issue, and I'm not sure they had the levers to fix it. Any provincial government might be able to bring a price down a bit, but governments can't have that level of impact to solve that problem. Still, the NDP hammered it as the BC Liberals' fault and Coleman took most of the blame."[183]

Coleman hopes that after the Cullen Commission final report, the public will believe that the people responsible for BC casinos did their best to identify and stop a handful of bad actors and actually had relatively positive outcomes while managing very challenging situations.

183 Interview with Keith Baldrey, December 7, 2023, by Zoom.

Chapter 30
LIFE AFTER POLITICS

*The man is a success who has lived well, laughed often,
and loved much; who has gained the respect of intelligent
men and the love of children; who has filled his niche and
accomplished his task; who leaves the world better than he
found it, whether by an improved poppy, a perfect poem, or a
rescued soul; who never lacked appreciation of earth's beauty
or failed to express it; who looked for the best in others and
gave the best he had.*

—Robert Louis Stevenson

Coleman is back to private business and consulting, occasionally getting involved in politics on an informal basis. Most of his life revolves around his family, and life is pretty good—except when he starts to follow what is happening in BC politics. Then he becomes a bit more intense in conversations, trying to see a solution to the problem in front of the free enterprise voters.

What is the lasting effect of the years of controversy on Rich Coleman and his legacy? I asked Coleman if he would meet my firefighter friend Allan Gregory for breakfast and take whatever questions he levelled at him. I told him in advance that Gregory was angry with him, which surprised Coleman because of the work he had done with firefighters. I explained it was about the last years in office. As a unique exercise, I invite the reader to sit in on that conversation, which took place at the Wedgewood Hotel on the morning of January 8, 2022.

Gregory: The name Coleman conjured up a real presence in politics, and our perception is formed through the media. Firefighters had 15-minute sessions with you but otherwise it's all sound bytes.

I appreciate your work on the cancer legislation, recognizing the toxicity of the job.

Mainly the name Coleman was the buffer between every problem and the BC Liberal government. Because you were able to deal with the media, you were always sent out and the "big dog" has a bark and a bit of a bite.

After all the years of seeing you in the news, I had to wonder, is Rich still a buffer? How much of the bathwater is he drinking?

Coleman: In 2001 when I was appointed to the position of solicitor general, the media said I was a loyal soldier who wouldn't amount to anything. Then 9/11 happened and I had to manage all of it immediately, and I did.

We were elected with 77 MLAs and everyone thought we should change the world, but the reality is we couldn't.

I was handed ICBC and told, 'Go fix that.' It wasn't that simple.

I felt like I was the fireman and was always sent to put out the fires. Sometimes it was frustrating.

I never avoided a scrum. I was always prepared to go out into the hall and talk about issues.

In the first few years, there was real media, properly researched stories. In the last three years we were in government, there was no money in the media, no research done. It all fell into a social media narrative.

Gregory: Casinogate was the big deal. Where things shifted was when pictures of bags of money were shown, and two things became obvious: First, that there was a massive influx of outside money and it was driving prices up, and second, that the housing market could be used to launder this money.

The public [was] left wondering, where is the accountability? Who was in control?

So many of our [firefighter] members were being forced to move further and further away from the city, being priced out of the housing market. The killer was the comment from Christy that there was no connection between foreign buyers and the cost of houses.

To the public, it was a complete dismissal of reality, and right in the midst of the other controversies.

Rich Coleman is the face of government. It doesn't matter what he is discussing, he is going to wear the whole issue.

Coleman: We were dealing with the Peter German report from the other side. I hired Rob Kroeker to do a report and a full scan of the allegations of illegal money.

German came in and did an interview at my Langley office. I was able to brief him on things that I can't talk about publicly. People don't understand that too much information at the wrong time will endanger someone's life. There was a loan shark operation, an investigation into the Hells Angels, a $500 million underground ring in Richmond that was leveraging local borrowing and tying it to people and families in China.

The Cullen Commission will never be able to touch the heart of these investigations. There's a real danger of people dying if anyone unravels the debt ring.

A government can only do so much. The single issue is not money laundering; it's a Supreme Court decision protecting lawyers' trust accounts.

We have no ability to see into the trust accounts. They can receive and transact and we can't prove anything. Lawyers don't have to disclose the origin of funds and their trusts are exempt from FINTRAC.

Gregory: The middle class is disappearing because we are being priced out of the housing market. Even firefighters who make a decent living and have stable jobs can't afford to be here anymore.

Coleman: I put in place a program for affordable housing in partnership with municipalities, the CMHC, and the private sector. It worked really well, with equity being returned to the local government when properties sell. The NDP killed the program when they were elected.

Gregory: The perception of the Christy Clark government is that you were not getting ahead of the media reports. The issues would mushroom and it felt like the government was not dealing with any of it.

The property transfer tax was paid to government. Follow the money. What was the incentive to deal with it when so much revenue was being paid in?

Christy denied that Asian money was causing the pricing increase.

The perception was that Christy liked the transfer tax cash cow and had no motivation to fix it.

You were all ignoring your fiduciary responsibility as a government to protect the voters.

The job market could not create jobs to support the new house prices.

People are already living pay cheque to pay cheque and falling behind. And the government doesn't care.

Communication was a huge issue. There was no commentary on any programs being offered to address the housing problem.

Christy's comment that there was no correlation was iconic and set the tone for the whole government.

When Rich Coleman came out to answer the media questions, it was as if the government was tone-deaf.

Who are they protecting in Point Grey? That's the question we are all asking.

Instead of Rich being the good lieutenant, the perception of Coleman is now wrapped up in the same dirt as the rest of the government.

The scandal became so big so fast it didn't matter who was speaking. It all sounded the same.

There may have been a gap between reality and perception.

It was interesting to see how many similarities there were between Gregory's observations and those of the Press Gallery veterans. After this breakfast, Coleman and Gregory developed a friendship, and I expect they may even work together on a project that supports First Responders with mental health and wellness. Gregory had considerable respect for Coleman for taking his questions, and a better understanding of the context for the controversies.

My hope with this book is that people will have access to Coleman's considerable legacy beyond the headlines.

Coleman said that the moment that he felt he was done with politics was when he went to the event for the Final Investment Decision for LNG Canada in October of 2018. This was the largest private sector investment in Canadian history, $40 billion dollars, the outcome of years of very hard, focused work.

John Horgan was premier at the time, quite ironic given how hard his party had fought against LNG. In his speech, he did not mention Christy Clark, instead giving all the credit to Coleman.

In the speeches, the prime minister recognized Coleman. Andy Calitz did an event with him and all the business people he knew from China were there. He said they all made a point of thanking him for his hard work in getting the project to the FID.

"They even put me in the picture with everybody at the event. They could have excluded me. I don't think they even invited Christy, and that was just wrong.

"I knew the NDP would try to take credit for it, and the federal government would. People were not fooled. They knew our government had done it."

Christy Clark confirmed that Horgan did not invite her to the event. She was disappointed but not surprised, given his past behaviour. However, she was very happy that the investment had finally been solidified and she gave huge credit to Coleman.

"I can't think of anyone who could have done that job better, or even as well, as Rich did. At times when it looked like things were going in the wrong direction, Rich kept the trains on the track. Investors were walking away from projects all over the world in 2014, and Rich kept investment interest in a high-cost situation. That was tough."

How does Coleman feel at the end of it all?

"I care and it hurts when people go after you. You can't let them know they are winning. They don't have to walk in your shoes. They have no clue how the job works.

"The fact is we made mistakes in the first four years, [which] made us look arrogant. It was tough because sometimes some of our guys were pretty arrogant and it reflects.

"I spent not less than 70 hours a week for 16 years as a cabinet minister. For me it was about serving the public. It was about the economy, jobs, [and] taxes. Especially after the last years of the NDP in the '90s somebody [had] to straighten [it] out."

Coleman's family is very proud and supportive of him, and his legacy of service has inspired his children and grandchildren. I spoke with his grandson Gabriel Johnson when Gabriel was 13 years old. His grandfather's work made a lasting impression on him, and the experiences were unique. "I remember watching him being elected and then he was anxious because he wasn't sure he was going to win. Then I remember my picture was in the paper, all of us hugging him, when he won.

"I am proud of him. I remember one time we were watching him, it was my mum [and] my cousin Andres, and we were all sitting around the television. When he was finished they all clapped, and then after granddad spoke, we all banged on the table the same way they did it in the legislature. I might think about going into politics, but it seems like a lot of stress, and all the things you have to go through, your input would only be a hand to vote ... I knew he was someone important, but he never made a big deal of it."[184]

His granddaughter Josephine Johnson, at 10 years old, had quite a bit to say about her grandfather as well, and made sure her grandfather had gifts that expressed her feelings. "Granddad—the man, the myth, the legend. If you had to give me three words for him, that's what was on the T-shirt we got him for Christmas a couple of years ago. My granddad is kind-hearted and warm-spirited. Cuddly. He's very funny and tells lots of good jokes.

"I have this one memory of him doing a speech, and then running into his arms after, and then he was holding me up for the whole crowd to see. I felt really important then. It was a place with a big tent and lots of chairs, at the annual BBQ that he always had.

"I remember when he put signs everywhere that said 'Vote for Rich Coleman,' and my cousins and I whenever we went to a park and saw one we would yell, 'YAY GRANDDAD!' This one day, Gabe and I were typing in names on the internet, we typed our names, our parents' names, and we finally got along to granddad, and then we started looking at all the pictures. We found this picture with him and little red horns on it and it said, 'Rich Coleman is the devil' and of course we knew that wasn't true.

---

184 Interview with Gabriel Johnson, March 18, 2022, in person.

"We know the true granddad so we would never believe something we saw on the internet about him that was wrong."[185]

Gabriel and Josephine's mom Jacqueline is Rich and Michele Coleman's daughter and works as a schoolteacher. "In truth, Dad will be there for anyone who needs help. I remember when he wanted to build a community centre, how he drew it on a piece of cardboard and that's how the idea started. From there, my mom and dad both jumped in to get it done, and we all became involved. The aspect of volunteering was so much a part of our family lives, and that just shifted over into politics after he was elected.

"I think his legacy is that he always managed to act with integrity and honesty. He had a reputation that if you called him, he would help. In the end, it's not about what you do in life, it's about how you make people feel when you are doing it.

"To see his reputation be questioned, tarnished, and have these things said about him... the people who know him and who are close to him know it's not true, but the problem is the media will really publicize the negative stories, but when it is corrected, if it is published at all, it is hard to find." [186]

Coleman's son Adam Coleman said, "My dad is a very stoic, honest, caring family man. He always tries to do right by the people he meets. I was around 12 years old when my dad first got into politics, my dad was involved in Kinsmen projects like the community centre... I remember events where we were the Kinkids and there were magic shows, pancake breakfasts... it was a real community, whether it was a bottle drive or going to a single mother's house to help with yard-work or dropping off a Christmas hamper."

During the 24 years that Coleman was elected, Adam saw the political world change through technology. "I'm quite thankful that the world didn't turn to social media until my adult years. I

185 Interview with Josephine Johnson, March 18, 2022, in person.
186 Interview with Jacqueline Johnson, May 15, 2021, by Zoom and email.

think it would have been quite difficult if social media had been around when I was a teenager. Kids these days have immediate access to the information, and teenagers can be quite cruel."

Adam remembers a key part of his father's legacy. "I think he did some really good work while he was solicitor general. Battling the first major BC forest fires in his time was part of it. What I remember specifically is it was the first time BC got its act together and enlisted the help of the Canadian military. I was a reserve soldier for 22 years. I was serving at that time. My employment didn't allow me to go, but I was very impressed with his ability to take that step and enlist that help. It is not an easy task and had never been done in our province before. It had been done in Manitoba for flooding and in Quebec for the ice storms. In BC we don't have a large regular force army contingent. It was all reserve soldiers. I was impressed with how quickly it happened—and keep in mind Canadian soldiers were not trained in how to fight forest fires—but he put together a two-week training program and they were certified. He was visiting the areas. He flew up with the premier. I was really proud of my dad."

As for the controversies around his dad? "It seemed there was a witch hunt specifically toward my dad. Knowing how hardworking [and] honest my father is, it was hurtful to read, it was hurtful to see. I didn't like what it was doing to him emotionally.

"I wish I could scream at the top of my lungs sometimes, 'You are dragging a good man's name through the mud and you are not telling his side of the story.' One thing my dad taught me and taught Jacqueline … is that not a lot of people will step forward to tell you that you are doing a good job. It seems there are many people who won't hesitate to criticize if you do anything wrong."

Adam sums up his dad's commitment this way, "It's not about the money, it's about doing a good job and making the province better for you, for your children, and for the future."

So what happens next in BC? As I finish this book, it feels like history is repeating itself in two ways. The first way was summed up by Keith Baldrey. "What we are seeing now is reminiscent of 1991. There are parallels, where the SoCreds virtually disappeared."

Baldrey is talking about the unprecedented move by BC Liberal Leader Kevin Falcon, who returned to politics after Andrew Wilkinson resigned, to take a second run at the leadership. He won this time. And then he led a name change for the BC Liberals so that they are now called BC United. Then, he kicked MLA John Rustad out of his caucus for comments he made about climate change. So Rustad became leader of the BC Conservative Party. As of January 2024, the BC Conservatives are rising in the polls and very few people know about BC United, although those who have heard the name think it is a soccer club.

"Biggest mistake the BC Liberals made was changing their name to BC United and kicking out John Rustad. Some of the NDP veterans are wary of the rise of the Conservatives, even though they like the split on the right."

Baldrey has watched enough elections in BC to know that sometimes the momentum can shift dramatically.

"if the vote split disappears, and the Conservatives become competitive, they could be a threat to the NDP. We could turn into a two-party province, with the Conservatives as the second party. The Greens are tanking. They are squeezed in a political sandwich. They are the forgotten part of the conversation. Unless they do something substantial, it is quite likely in the next election, the Green Party will be vanquished."

The BC Liberals have vanished from the political landscape, just as the BC Conservative Party did in 1933 when Simon Fraser Tolmie changed the name to the Unionist Party, opening the door to the Liberals taking the place of the Conservatives in the next election. Is this a karmic return?

And which political party will Rich Coleman be supporting in October 2024?

The last word goes to Keith Baldrey. "Coleman will be remembered as one of the most prominent faces of 16 years of BC Liberal government. You take on a profile that is pretty permanently etched on the landscape. If you think of Campbell and Christy Clark, you remember Coleman, de Jong, and Bond. He will be remembered for his permanency in government. You have to go back to Wacky for that length of service. He was an ongoing member of cabinet in senior positions. He was solicitor general; he was forests; he was housing; and he was high-profile as solicitor general."[187]

---

187 Interview with Keith Baldrey, December 7, 2023, by Zoom.

Appendix A
CABINET RESPONSIBILITIES

Rich Coleman Cabinet Responsibilities, Major Agencies, Boards and Commissions, 2001 to 2017[188]
Summary of Responsibilities—June 5, 2001
Public Safety and Solicitor General
General Responsibilities

- Police and correctional services

- Youth corrections

- Sexual assault centres and women's assault centres

- Film classification

- Liquor control and licensing

- Gaming policy and enforcement

- Consumer legislation and investigations

- Landlord-tenant dispute resolution

- Travel agent operations

- Cemetery operations

---

188 Courtesy of Erika Luebbe, Manager, Reference Services, Legislative
    Library of British Columbia, Victoria, BC, December 31, 2021, by email.

Major Agencies, Boards, and Commissions

- Police boards
- BC Parole Board
- BC Police Commission
- Commercial Appeals Commission
- BC Lottery Corporation
- BC Racing Commission
- BC Coroners Service
- Motion Picture Appeal Board
- Travel Assurance Board
- Liquor Appeal Board

Summary of Ministerial Responsibilities—June 16, 2005
MINISTRY OF FORESTS AND RANGE (and Minister Responsible for Housing)
General Responsibilities

- Forest stewardship and timber supply
- Forest protection—pests and fire
- Compliance and enforcement
- Forest investment
- Timber pricing and sales
- BC timber sales
- Grazing and range stewardship
- Housing and homelessness policy

Major Agencies, Boards, and Commissions

- Forest Appeals Commission

- Forest Practices Board

- Forestry Innovation Investments Ltd.

- Timber Export Advisory Committee

- BC Housing Management Commission

- Premier's Taskforce on Homelessness

Summary of Ministry Responsibilities—June 23, 2008
MINISTRY OF HOUSING AND SOCIAL DEVELOPMENT
General Responsibilities

- Housing and homeless policy

- Building policy

- Safety standards and inspections

- Landlord-tenant dispute resolution

- Income assistance programs

- Employment assistance programs

- Disability assistance

- Adult Community Living Services

- Transition houses

- Mental health and addictions services coordination

- Community access grants and volunteer support

- Liquor control and licensing

- Gaming policy

- Responsible Gaming Strategy

Major Agencies, Boards, and Commissions

- Building Code Appeal Board
- Building Policy Advisory Committee
- Homeowner Protection Office
- Residential Tenancy Office
- Safety Standards Appeal Board
- Safety Authority of BC
- BC Housing Management Commission
- Provincial Rental Housing Commission
- BC Lottery Corporation
- Liquor Distribution Branch
- Community Living BC

Coleman Appointed Solicitor General—April 27, 2009
Responsibilities include oversight of policing, corrections, and the provincial emergency program. Coleman also retains his duties as Minister of Housing and Social Development.

Summary of Ministry Responsibilities—June 10, 2009
MINISTRY OF HOUSING AND SOCIAL DEVELOPMENT
General Responsibilities

- Housing and homeless policy
- Building policy
- Safety standards and inspections
- Landlord-tenant dispute resolution
- Income assistance

- Disability assistance
- Delivery of employment programs
- Provincial Disability Strategy
- Adult community living services
- Transition houses
- Mental health and addictions services coordination
- Volunteer and non-profit support
- Liquor control and licensing
- Liquor Distribution Branch
- Gaming policy
- Responsible Gambling Strategy
- Community gaming grants

Major Agencies, Boards, and Commissions
- BC Housing Management Commission
- BC Lottery Corporation
- Community Living BC
- Building Code Appeal Board
- Homeowner Protection Office
- Building Policy Advisory Committee
- Safety Standards Appeal Board
- Safety Authority of BC
- Provincial Rental Housing Commission

Summary of Ministry Responsibilities—October 25, 2010

MINISTRY OF PUBLIC SAFETY AND SOLICITOR GENERAL (Minister Responsible for Housing)

Minister of State for Building Code Renewal

General Responsibilities

- Police and correctional services

- Provincial emergency management

- Emergency social services

- Crime prevention programs

- Criminal record check and protection order registry

- Victim assistance

- Consumer services

- Superintendent of Motor Vehicles

- Office of the Fire Commissioner

- Housing and homeless policy

- Transition houses

- Building policy

- Safety standards and inspections

- Landlord-tenant dispute resolution

- Liquor control and licensing

- Liquor Distribution Branch

- Gaming policy and enforcement

- Responsible Gambling Strategy

- Community gaming grants

Major Agencies, Boards, and Commissions

- Insurance Corporation of British Columbia

- Police boards

- BC Coroners Service

- BC Housing Management Commission

- BC Lottery Corporation

- Building Code Appeal Board

- Homeowner Protection Office

- Building Policy Advisory Committee

- Safety Standards Appeal Board

- Safety Authority of BC

- Provincial Rental Housing Corporation

Summary of Ministry Responsibilities—March 14, 2011
MINISTRY OF ENERGY AND MINES (Minister Responsible for Housing)
General Responsibilities

- Electricity and alternative energy policy

- Oil and gas policy

- Offshore oil and gas policy

- Energy efficiency

- Renewable energy development

- Innovative Clean Energy Fund

- Mines and minerals policy

- Permitting and inspections of major mining projects

- Geological Survey Service
- Housing and homeless policy
- Transition houses
- Building policy
- Safety standards and inspections
- Landlord–tenant dispute resolution

Major Agencies, Boards, and Commissions

- BC Hydro and Power Authority
- Columbia Power Corporation
- Oil and Gas Commission
- BC Housing Management Commission
- Building Code Appeal Board
- Homeowner Protection Office
- Building Policy Advisory Committee
- Safety Standards Appeal Board
- Safety Authority of BC
- Provincial Rental Housing Corporation

September 5, 2012
MINISTRY OF ENERGY, MINES and NATURAL GAS
(Minister Responsible for Housing)
General Responsibilities

- Electricity and alternative energy policy
- Oil and gas policy

- Offshore oil and gas policy
- Energy efficiency
- Renewable energy development
- Innovative Clean Energy Fund
- Mines and minerals policy
- Mineral and coal titles
- Permitting and inspections of major mining projects
- Geological Survey Service
- Housing and homeless policy
- Transition houses
- Building policy
- Safety standards and inspections
- Landlord-tenant dispute resolution
- Liquor control and licensing
- Liquor Distribution Branch
- Gaming policy and enforcement
- Responsible Gambling Strategy

Major Agencies, Boards, and Commissions
- BC Hydro and Power Authority
- Columbia Power Corporation
- Oil and Gas Commission
- BC Housing Management Commission
- Building Code Appeal Board

- Homeowner Protection Office
- Building Policy Advisory Committee
- Safety Standards Appeal Board
- Safety Authority of BC
- Provincial Rental Housing Corporation
- BC Lottery Corporation
- Pavilion Corporation of BC

Summary of ministry responsibilities—June 10, 2013
MINISTRY OF NATURAL GAS DEVELOPMENT (Minister Responsible for Housing)
General Responsibilities

- Oil and gas policy
- Liquid Natural Gas (LNG)
- Oil and gas pipelines
- Housing and homeless policy
- Transition houses
- Building policy
- Safety standards and inspections
- Landlord-tenant dispute resolution

Major Agencies, Boards, and Commissions

- Oil and Gas Commission
- BC Housing Management Commission
- Building Code Appeal Board

- Building Policy Advisory Committee

- Safety Standards Appeal Board

- British Columbia Safety Authority

- Provincial Rental Housing Corporation

Ministry responsibilities—June 12, 2017
MINISTRY OF ENERGY AND MINES (Minister Responsible
for Core Review)
General Responsibilities

- Electricity and alternative energy policy

- Energy efficiency

- Renewable energy development

- Innovative Clean Energy Fund

- Mines and minerals permitting and inspections except for
major mining projects

- Mines and minerals policy

- Mineral and coal titles

- Permitting and inspections of major mining projects

- BC Geological Survey

- Core Review

Major Agencies, Boards, and Commissions

- BC Hydro and Power Authority

- Columbia Power Corporation

- Columbia Basin Trust

Index

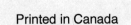

Printed in Canada